Pilgrimages

Pilgrimages

ASPECTS OF JAPANESE LITERATURE AND CULTURE

J. Thomas Rimer

UNIVERSITY OF HAWAII PRESS

HONOLULU

93 92 91 90 89 88   5 4 3 2 1

Publication of this book has
been assisted by a grant from
the Japan Foundation.

Library of Congress Cataloging-in-Publication Data

Rimer, J. Thomas.
  Pilgrimages : aspects of Japanese literature and culture / J.
Thomas Rimer.
      p.   cm.
  Bibliography: p.
  Includes index.
  ISBN 0-8248-1148-8
  1,   Japanese literature—History and criticism. 2.   Art, Japanese-
European influences. 3.   Theater—Japan. 4.   Pilgrims and
pilgrimages in literature. I.   Title.
PL715.R56   1988   88-21621
895.6'09—dc19   CIP

for Suzanne,
my French connection

Contents

Introduction

When I was an undergraduate my favorite, and arguably my wisest, professor convinced me that the art of reading, and by extension the art of any active response to knowledge, lies in the area of making connections. Sensing the unseen ties and patterns that can connect individual works of art together, and so eventually link them to the reader or spectator, brings, he assured me, the core of that special and crucial pleasure that the arts contribute to our lives. His remarks touched a strong chord of response in me. This collection of essays pays homage, if nothing more, to that youthful ideal. Certainly those of us who work in Japanese studies are faced with the buried existence of a number of artistic and cultural assumptions— about the nature of art, the purposes of verbal communication, and the place of literature in cultural life, among others—that make our understanding and interpretation of Japanese texts both an agreeably demanding and a sometimes problematic adventure. A variety of hidden assumptions lies not only behind the individual works we read, but in our own minds as well, for we bring our own unarticulated expectations, preconceptions, and prejudices about the nature and purposes of literature to our attempts to decipher the works with which we engage ourselves.

In the case of the Japanese tradition, a certain number of assumptions shared by Japanese writers and readers suggest sufficient congruences with our own modern Western ideas of literature that we risk being lulled into a complacent transposition into our own terms of material that is, in the most exciting sense of the word, alien. We run the risk of domestication when we might better be pushing ourselves to grasp what the works under study really represent and how they function.

If we are to read Japanese works of literature in their own contexts, then, what critical terms might prove most useful? Traditional
Japanese methodologies of analysis, like the works they seek to interpret, often work on principles that do not provide the most useful
bridge to understanding for contemporary Western readers; they are
a transposition of the problem, a metamorphosis that may not bring
the work much closer. Modern Japanese criticism, on the other
hand, sometimes shows an important degree of influence from Western models of criticism, revealing a level of cosmopolitanism roughly
equivalent to the best of the modern Japanese literary works themselves, where the influences of Western literature have also been crucial. Those modern linkages allow us, I believe, to make use in turn
of certain Western critical methods, which, if applied modestly and
with some common sense, can prove genuinely useful in analyzing
Japanese literature. Such, at least, is the case I attempt to argue in
this small book.

By way of an example let me indicate one instance of what I would
identify as an important but unarticulated assumption that lies
beneath the surface of many Japanese literary texts. This strategy
might be identified as a movement, a trajectory away from any realism in the contemporary (or indeed the classical) American sense,
into a realm of heightened poetic sensibility. I have come to believe
that in this regard the actual words that compose the texts of such
works are ordered to serve as a means to induce this state rather than
to serve as ends in themselves. In pursuing this insight I have been
aided in particular by the work of the anthropologist Victor Turner,
whose observations on the dynamics of pilgrimage and whose understanding of the mechanisms that can achieve spiritual displacement
have been of inspiration in the development of my own thinking.

Most of these essays began as lectures. Re-created in written form
over a period of several years, they betray their origins by their sim-
plicity of language, their suggestiveness, and their exploratory
nature. Perhaps much of what I have written may seem more sketch
than finished picture; yet while more details and arguments might
have been provided, I have preferred to consider each of these essays
as a probe rather than as a statement. Since, as I have suggested
above, critical methodologies appropriate to Western views of Japanese literature are still being developed, I prefer suggestions to dic-
tums at our present stage of inquiry.

A final word of critical vocabulary. Terms used in a number of different methodologies found in European, Japanese, and American critical theory turn up here and there in these essays. There is little reference, however, to the most recent of French fashions, despite the Continental connections discussed in a number of the essays. There is good reason for this, at least so far as I am concerned. A colleague of mine in the field of comparative literature said to me a year or two ago, "We can deconstruct Flaubert because we have been at such pains to *construct* him, sometimes well, sometimes poorly, for the last seventy years." Japanese literary studies have not, in my opinion, yet reached this stage. I still find myself attempting to call up in some useful fashion the assumptions that lie beneath the texts I read. It will take sharper minds than mine and perhaps another generation of scholarship before those assumptions, once identified, can themselves be—if indeed they need be—called into question.

The preparation of this study has given me a great deal of pleasure, particularly as I was able to receive so much good advice from a number of friends and colleagues. In particular I would like to thank Stuart Kiang and Patricia Crosby of the University of Hawaii Press, who did such a thorough and imaginative job of editing the manuscript. I am grateful as well to my two readers, who made a number of judicious suggestions and gently pointed out some errors which, I hope, have now been satisfactorily corrected. The Japan Foundation kindly supplied transparencies for the paintings by Umehara Ryūzaburo, Saeki Yūzō, and Hasegawa Toshiyuki. The color printing was assisted by a generous grant from the General Research Board of the Graduate School, University of Maryland, College Park. Finally, I would like to thank Ms. Eriko Kishida for permission to publish the English translation of the Kishida play *Buranko,* included in chapter 3.

I
THE SEARCH
FOR A SPECIAL FELICITY

Five Japanese in Paris

1

Aware on the Seine
Shimazaki Tōson Reads Bashō

I met a traveller from an antique land
Who said: Two vast and trunkless legs of stone
Stand in the desert . . . Near them, on the sand,
Half sunk, a shattered visage lies, whose frown,
And wrinkled lip, and sneer of cold command,
Tell that its sculptor well those passions read
Which yet survive, stamped on these lifeless things,
The hand that mocked them, and the heart that fed:
And on the pedestal these words appear:
"My name is Ozymandias, king of kings:
Look on my works, ye Mighty, and despair!"
Nothing beside remains. Round the decay
Of that colossal wreck, boundless and bare
The lone and level sands stretch far away.

Shelley, *Ozymandias*

AMERICANS, perhaps better than any others, ought to have a sympathy, and so perhaps an understanding, of the profound attraction that one culture can feel for another. American culture has been molded by the dialectic of our continuing relationship with the development of European civilization, and much of our developing and changing self-image has come from our own sense of a response to the Other, a model to be emulated or discarded but never altogether ignored. We are less aware, perhaps, of the profound relationship that Japanese artists and intellectuals have felt with France. The fascination that the French felt for Japan, particularly for her arts, in the latter part of the nineteenth century has been well documented, but relatively little has been written about the continuing excitement that the French intellectual, social, and artistic model has supplied for Japan since roughly the same period. A list of the important writers and intellectuals from the interwar period will show at once how powerful these affinities were to become: Yokomitsu Riichi the novelist, Nishiwaki Junzaburō the poet, Saeki Yūzō and half a dozen other important artists, Kuki Shūzō the philosopher, and many others spent much of

3

their professional and creative lives trying to place in the context of their own evolving sense of Japanese civilization the lessons they felt that they had learned through the French experience.

Yet what was the nature of those lessons? Any narrow examination of influences, in any very literal sense of the word, would seem to suggest that at least in the best cases the results of the encounter between these two artistic and intellectual worlds cannot simply be described in terms of copying or imitation. Here too the comparison between the American and the Japanese reactions to Europe in the nineteenth and early twentieth centuries are worth noting. Many Americans felt, in the manner of a Henry James, that they wanted to add to their personal integrity (and so perhaps to their national identity) a sense of history and culture that their own immediate environment seemed unable to provide. Most Japanese intellectuals, however, went to Europe with at least a nascent sense of the fact that they represented a civilization with its own culture and traditions; they were not going to Europe *for* culture but as people of culture seeking to know the world.

There are many points in the history of these growing cultural connections at which a reader can observe the growth of these attitudes and distinctions among the Japanese who went to France. One of them is certainly to be found in the observations of the novelist Nagai Kafū, whose visit to France from 1907 through 1908 (after a five-year period in the United States) helped form not only his own view of the way in which French and Japanese cultures functioned but, through his writings, helped establish him both as something of an apostle of French culture and as a powerful critic of what he saw to be the shortcomings in the development of his own country. Kafū felt strongly that a traditional sense of wholeness was being eaten away by a lack of self-conscious appreciation for the real virtues of Japanese civilization. Kafū's attitudes have been well explored in an elegant and eloquent book by Edward Seidensticker, *Kafū the Scribbler*,[1] and so do not need to be repeated here. But the example of Shimazaki Tōson (1872–1943), a figure perhaps even more revered, and read, in his own day and since than Kafū, can provide another alternative and revealing model of the way in which a perceived natural cultural affinity on the part of one gifted Japanese novelist came to work itself out in the course of an actual visit. Tōson's trip and his responses as he recorded them came to serve later generations as partial models of what the appropriate Japanese responses might be. Later writers, such as Yokomitsu, quoted Tōson's writings on France in their own. Tōson's responses allowed him to become an inadvertent role model, a guide for those who would follow. Tōson, of course, did not create this interest in France any more than did Kafū, and it is not my goal here to trace the development of the attraction from its very beginnings. By the time of Tōson's generation, it seemed a safe assumption that France was a country of high civilization, a *bunmeikoku,* and that a visit there would provide a sensitive visitor with a higher and broader sense of the meaning of human experience and Japan's own place in human history.

Looking over what Tōson wrote during and subsequent to his trip concerning his French years suggests a number of means by which his experience can be evaluated. From the vantage point of our present generation, it would seem that the most useful attitudes his writings reveal cluster about three areas: the stance of the artist, the view that an artist should take of his own work, and the meaning that art should have for an artist. To all these concerns Tōson speaks eloquently, often poignantly. Before explicating the general thrust of these attitudes, however, it should be pointed out that Tōson had himself inherited a number of cultural assumptions about the arts and their functioning from the long classical tradition in which he was educated. Tōson's own writings indicate his debt to these conceptions. Perhaps the best place to find an eloquent summation of these older attitudes is in certain statements made to his students by the great poet Matsuo Bashō (1644–1694). Bashō's aesthetic represents in many ways the summation of traditional insights into the functioning of the creative process as it relates to poetic language. Then too, Tōson himself, as will be clear later, was, like so many of his fellow writers and artists, a great admirer of Bashō, regarding him as the outstanding writer of *haiku* poetry during the Tokugawa period (1600–1868).

Bashō, of course, had many things to say about the nature of art and the artist, but three convictions he expressed are especially evocative in terms of Tōson's own experience. The first of them has to do with what might be termed a kind of poetic empathy: the artist must seek his inspiration in the life he finds around him, in objects and incidents which he can witness himself and with which he can find some sort of artistic identification.

What is important is to keep our mind high in the world of true understanding, and returning to the world of our daily experience to seek therein the truth of beauty. No matter what we may be doing at a given moment, we must not forget that it has a bearing on our everlasting self which is poetry.[2]

A close observation of nature can allow the kind of intimate identification and spiritual consonance that can give birth to the possibility of a creative act.

Go to the pine if you want to learn about the pine, or to the bamboo if you want to learn about the bamboo. . . . However well phrased your poetry may be, if your feeling is not natural—if the object and yourself are separate—then your poetry is not true poetry but merely your subjective counterfeit.[3]

Combined with this grounding in the specificity of nature is another attitude valued by Bashō, a sort of transcendental yearning for some quality of experience that lies outside the everyday experience of life, a quality that can bring closer a distant and intuited sense of some larger emotional, even philosophical reality. This quality might be described as a kind of longing (*akogare* in Japanese) on a spiritual level. This sense of yearning pushes the artist toward the impulse to seek something beyond his own immediate and familiar responses to life. This yearning is related in turn to the classical literary virtue of *aware,* a Japanese term difficult to translate directly but which might be described as a deep sensitivity to the world that can permit the writer to grasp the fundamental power and deep significance of life, felt as a truly personal response to an incident, perhaps a trifling one, from his or her daily life. It was surely a sense of the central need for developing these instincts in himself that led Bashō to become a wanderer. In his *Records of a Travel-worn Satchel,* based on his travels of 1687 and 1688, Bashō came as close as he was ever to do in writing a paragraph of spiritual autobiography, and his statements are couched in just such terms.

In this mortal frame of mine which is made of a hundred bones and nine orifices there is something, and this something is called a windswept spirit for lack of a better name, for it is much like a thin drapery that is torn and swept away at the slightest stir of the wind. This some-

thing in me took to writing poetry years ago, merely to amuse itself at
first, but finally making it its lifelong business. . . . yet indeed ever
since it began to write poetry it has never found peace with itself,
always wavering between doubts of one kind or another . . . the fact
is, it knows no other art than the art of writing poetry and therefore
hangs onto it more or less blindly.[4]

The poetic vocation thus includes a yearning, one which can easily
translate itself into spatial terms, as Bashō explicates so clearly in the
famous opening paragraph of his *Narrow Road to the Deep North*.

Days and months are the travellers of eternity. So are the years that
pass by. Those who steer a boat across the sea, or drive a horse across
the earth till they succumb to the weight of years, spend every minute
of their lives travelling. I myself have been tempted for a long time by
the cloud-moving wind—filled with a strong desire to wander.[5]

Seeking for enlightenment beyond the immediate milieu of one's
prior personal experience goes back in turn to such eminent cultural
models as the Buddhist poet Saigyō (1118–1190), who abandoned the
life of the court for that of the wandering poet-recluse, and he too has
his antecedents in such powerful if shadowy literary figures as the
priest Nōin (c. 1000). The connections between displacement and
enlightenment were established early in Japanese culture and it is
therefore not surprising that such models would continue to resonate
in the modern period.

Seeking another level of experience often provided as well the possibility of using another culture as a point of reference. For Bashō, of
course, that point of reference was China. In case after case, Bashō is
able to reveal his emotional and artistic individuality through references to Chinese literature, particularly to the poetry of the great
T'ang poet Tu Fu, or to the geography of the famous scenes in China
that had inspired her writers and poets. Beauty in Japan was often
traditionally defined in the shadow of such Chinese standards,
although Bashō was never able to witness such scenes himself.
Indeed, the attitudes of *akogare,* until the present century, were often
based on an unarticulated assumption that the object of adoration
would *not* be experienced, but only imagined.

If Bashō remained at home, Tōson lived in another time and it was
possible for him to go to France. Unlike many of his compatriots in

the field of the arts and literature, however, Tōson made the journey not as a student but as a mature artist; he went less to learn than to observe, less to seek an opening out than to find an escape from a difficult personal emotional situation in which he found himself at home. Tōson left for France in 1913 and remained until 1915, and so witnessed both the richness of the end of the prewar period and the difficulties of France under wartime conditions. However complicated Tōson's personal life and interior state of mind may have been at the time of his departure, there was no question but that France was a goal that he consciously sought. When asked why he had chosen Paris, he quoted in his writings a statement he had read to the effect that "Paris is the capital of the arts, the fountainhead of culture, the center of fashion, and the hub of elegant behavior." For him there could be no other choice.

Tōson wrote three books about his French experience, and the reader can gain a good grasp of the meaning of France to Tōson by examining and juxtaposing these texts together. They divide up in a most arresting way Tōson's various concerns. The first of them, *Paris dayori* (News from Paris), is a series of articles and other communications collected together and published in book form in 1915. These pieces might be considered as representing the intellectual side of Tōson's visit. *Étranger,* a reworking of much of this material, published in 1922, puts more of an emphasis on social relationships and personal speculations. Finally Tōson's novel *Shinsei* (New Life), published in 1919, represents his artistic treatment of the trip and its emotional implications for him as an artist. These texts must be juxtaposed because in none of them does Tōson explore all three aspects of his response. Indeed, his division of the material is reminiscent of the courtiers in the Heian period who wrote their matter-of-fact diaries in classical Chinese and their more personal, introspective thoughts in the classical form of thirty-one-syllable *waka* poetry. This psychological split was carried on in the modern period too, for example, in the writing of a novelist like Mori Ōgai, whose diaries written during his stay in Germany chronicle in the driest and most unemotional way most of his encounters, while his fictionalized pieces show with great skill his emotional involvements and spiritual perplexities. Unusual as this split may appear in terms of Western analogues, writers in the Japanese tradition seem comfortable with such division. Indeed, in the case of Yokomitsu Riichi and his visit to

France, his novel *Ryoshū* (The Sadness of Travel), mentioned above, often sinks under the very weight of trying to mix his personal, intellectual, and social concerns.

News from Paris shows to what extent Tōson was able to penetrate into French life. He describes various French and Japanese he was able to meet, discusses the sightseeing possibilities he came to enjoy with his Baedeker's guide, and chronicles his admiration for such French writers as Flaubert and Maupassant. Like so many tourists before and after, he finds himself frustrated at the problems he encounters in speaking French, and seeks out a tutor to help him learn to communicate. He visits the theatre and the opera, and goes to concerts with his visiting colleague Osanai Kaoru, who has just returned from a visit to Moscow to attend performances at the Moscow Art Theatre. Osanai, several years before, had opened his famous Free Theatre in Tokyo and was the intellectual and artistic force behind the movement for a modern theatre in Japan; Tōson was thus conversant with, and sympathetic toward, the best and newest artistic trends in France. That much is clear as well from the conversations he reports with various Japanese painters he knew while in France. Tōson experienced the best of what was happening, and seemed to take genuine pleasure from all he saw and heard.

In the course of his artistic and intellectual investigations, Tōson poses and then takes up a number of questions that he felt were of intellectual importance to him and to other Japanese as well. Four of them may be mentioned here. The first concerned the image of Japan that he found prevalent in France, and, by implication, in Europe generally.

> My friend was told by a Russian colleague that "Russia herself was only comprehended in Europe after her arts were understood." Japan is only known in the world because of her victory in the Russo-Japanese War: such was the sole boast made by so many of our countrymen, and we who come to Europe are still haunted by that ghost. The fact that we too are made of flesh and blood, that we too live, love, and die, is not truly understood here. We have not as yet truly joined our hands together.[6]

In a series of remarks scattered throughout the volume, Tōson develops his conviction that the best, perhaps the only way to penetrate another culture is through her arts.

As a traveller in a foreign land, I have come to realize again and again the supreme value of the arts. I am deeply convinced that if two disparate peoples wish to understand each other, really wish to grasp each other's point of view, there is no straighter, no surer road than through the arts.[7]

A third related issue about which Tōson shows concern involves the question of the attitude that Japan should take toward the West in terms of her own development as a civilization. Tōson finds that these questions concern many of the Japanese he meets, and he paraphrases their remarks, often with striking effect. A professor from Tokyo University, for example, tells him:

I don't see how we can be satisfied with the simplistic attitude that Japan at this time need expend her efforts only to surpass European civilization. It is not possible for us to become Europeans. If we are not convinced that Japan has her own unique culture, a culture that is different from that of Europe, then our own authenticity simply vanishes away.[8]

An artist tells him:

The Japanese are too quick to take on and adapt other models. When Chinese culture was introduced into Japan, we tried to hurry to the level of the Chinese; now, in the case of European culture, we rush to attempt the same thing. This seems to represent some sort of national trait. And we often seem capable of no more than that. For just these reasons we adopted Chinese characters, so ill suited for our own language, and we haven't been able to escape them since. Why are we in such a hurry to adopt these other models? Why didn't we develop a system of writing more appropriate to our own language?[9]

The artist proposes no answer to his rhetorical question, but Tōson, in a later passage, goes on to suggest a response that is both thoughtful and moving.

What is a copy? Here in Paris there are many copies of things that have been made in Asia. Whatever could be collected from all over the world has been brought here, and copied, in order to make life richer and more abundant. Annam, India, Egypt, all these civilizations are copied a great deal. Yet these countries do not have the strength themselves to copy. Indeed, multiplicity is no cause for grief when choosing a model. The source of concern is rather that the strength to copy will be unequal to the task. If that strength is not resolute enough, if the copy is indifferent, or halfhearted, then the real thing that is being copied can never truly become one's own.[10]

Here, it would seem, is a first echo in Tōson of Bashō's conviction, mentioned above, that "if the object and yourself are separate—then your poetry is not true poetry but merely your subjective counterfeit." This attitude, which has served as a literary virtue in traditional Japan, now seems, at least to some of Tōson's colleagues, to pose a series of difficulties (some at least attributable to the Modernist movement everywhere), but Tōson remains resolute in his conviction that art can only be created through a process of identification and internalization.

Finally, Tōson takes great delight in his discovery that the French, when they talk of Impressionism in art and music, are actually in touch with many vital principles that in fact make up the great Japanese traditions. In this sense Tōson reverses the discoveries made two decades or more before by French artists who sensed affinities with Japan through her woodblock prints and other artifacts. Tōson finds in the concert hall that he somehow possesses an immediate and gratifying grasp of the music of Debussy, which still was such a puzzlement to many of his French contemporaries. He comments:

> Perhaps from early times our artists have been somehow equipped with a powerful ability to create a kind of Impressionism. We have all been born with a taste for such Impressionism . . . I am certainly not suggesting that there is in fact any connection between the exoticism of contemporary Western music and our own; still, I must say that, as I am listening to Debussy, I somehow feel that I might be listening to one of our own *nagauta* artists. Therefore, just as some old *waka* or *haiku* written long ago may actually still move us, so some ancient classic popular ballad can still entice our spirits. Is there no modern musician who can save Japanese music from mere entertainers, that old music that can convey to us the sights of those who harbored and loved the very laments of the insects in the fall?[11]

Making the cultural rounds in Paris, Tōson visited many museums and developed a continuing interest in French art, particularly that of the nineteenth and early twentieth centuries. His favorite was Cézanne, then coming to be so appreciated in France after a period of neglect, and he shared most of his contemporaries' attraction to Rodin. The appeal of certain other artists escaped him, and he found himself particularly puzzled over the attraction others felt to Delacroix and Puvis de Chavannes. Tōson travelled all over the city, and his sense of the beauty of his surroundings was conveyed through his appreciative and astute remarks concerning the city planning evident in the arrangement of the Paris streets, and in particular the skillful use of garden spaces in urban design. Concerning this point he made a number of evocative comparisons between the role of gardens in France and in Japan.

In the midst of all this objective observation and appreciation of his surroundings, Tōson allowed a certain unsettling subjectivity to emerge, containing elements that had more to do with his inner state of mind; it was clear that he felt somehow cut off, that his life was shrinking in its potential. He had hoped to seek and find some kind of rebirth in France, and the period was proving an unexpectedly difficult one for him. These concerns are considerably more evident in *Étranger,* in which he discusses his personal relationships with those he had come to know in Paris, particularly his Japanese friends. Concerning them, and himself, his speculations become considerably more personal than in *News from Paris.*

I realize now that I have passed a year here, I, who came to this far place in order to forget everything. Did I, in fact, come to this land about which I knew nothing in order to separate myself from my own country; or did I come here in order to discover my own country? I can no longer make the distinction. I know I could not have lived one day without Japan.[12]

Musing on the nature of travel and its psychological significance for the traveller, Tōson reflects on the significance to him of his relatively quiet existence in Paris.

Among the travellers I have observed, my colleagues who travel in foreign countries seem to move about a great deal. There seem few indeed who, like me, have not changed their lodgings or who have stayed for a long time in one place. My whole method of travel differs from that of these others; for one reason, I thought to live near an agreeable teacher of French. In the end I wanted to make a trip with the same mental attitude that I have when I travel in my own country. I wished to have no special sensation of travelling in a *foreign* country.[13]

Tōson speculates on his family; he is haunted by the reality of separation. The reader of *Étranger* moves closer to Tōson the man, and the confusion of soul that he openly chronicles is truly touching.

A strange vision entered into my dreams. Since coming to France, I have seldom been possessed by such a dream.

It was a day in May; the weather seemed uncertain, as though it were slipping back from spring. The cold rain I saw ran off the young leaves sprouting on the *platanes*. I found myself exhausted from a long trip and had been stretched out since the afternoon on my bed.

Suddenly I was walking in the grounds of an ancient temple in the country. Within those grounds there was a small building that could be rented out, an arrangement not to be found among the churches in Paris. With a sense of profound surprise I found myself walking on the soil of my own land, and after such a long time; and then I was suddenly surrounded by children. Surprisingly enough they were French children. One pushed his way over to peer closely at my face. Another followed behind me in amazement. Why such a sense of wonder? Because I was walking about in Japanese clothes. Because they had caught a glimpse, for the first time, of a custom that was purely Japanese.

When I awoke, I found myself, of course, in a hotel, here in this far-off land. At the end of this voyage of almost three years, such was the dream that I had. Things from my country, things from here in France, seemed inexplicably intermixed, and a feeling of confusion that came over me did not easily depart, even long after I awakened. Somehow, Japan seemed further and further from me.[14]

These sorts of emotional states are best and most evocatively described in the novel *A New Life,* in which they become the focus of the structure of the entire voyage of the protagonist, Kishimoto. The book is an account of faith and renewal, and religious imagery plays an important part in the linguistic strategies of the text. These emotional layers as revealed in Kishimoto's interior monologues indicate that indeed *A New Life* is a *roman à clef;* Tōson is Kishimoto, and his novel reveals, and, as some contemporary critics felt, in unseemly detail, one set of reasons for Tōson's desire to travel abroad—in order to escape from a sentimental and sexual relationship with his niece, who became pregnant with his child. However close to the events in Tōson's life the novel may be, it certainly reads to our generation as an authentic work of art, in which the emotional trajectory of travel as loss and renewal is rendered with dignity and intensity. The seriousness of the journey for Kishimoto is suggested early in the book, when he comes to realize that his voyage, begun as an escape, inevitably becomes a journey to an as yet cloudy destination.

Kishimoto had made a decision that the trip was unavoidable; but although he had merely thought to remove himself from a difficult situation, he now found himself making a comparison with the religious convert for whom one feels compassion, the one who throws everything away, who "abandons the burning house."[15]

He soon comes to realize, however, that travel is a crucial part of the process by which one comes to recognize oneself as a stranger, the first of a series of long steps that will lead to self-renewal.

> Kishimoto realized not only that he was a traveller, but that he was a foreigner as well. He remembered the unconscious naturalness with which he had walked the streets of Tokyo, like a fish from the sea content with his habitat; there, when he saw the rare visitor from another country, he would think to himself, "There goes a foreigner." Now the situation was reversed. It was not merely his own consciousness that his hair was of a different color, as was the color of his skin, but that the contours of his face were different, that the very irises of his eyes were another shade. Everyone who met him stared at him intently. To be put in such a position of constantly being observed made him nervous each time he ventured out.[16]

Kishimoto begins to lose his sense of time and his sharp response to the exterior world. "Everyone on a trip is involved in suffering," he tells himself, and begins, during his wanderings in Paris and later in the countryside around the city, to seek out some means of repentance and renewal. At this stage of his pilgrimage, Kishimoto learns that travel can bring rebirth as well, the "new life" that he has been seeking. His new level of consciousness is created in a central passage that describes his reactions to the beauty of the countryside of France.

Kishimoto walked through a field of growing vegetables behind the farmhouse. He continued along a narrow path that ran through the middle, looking at the fruit trees planted on both sides. It was a spot, like the pasture, where he usually came for a rest, where he would often pick a peach off a branch to enjoy its taste, where he could walk about with the smell of the earth in his nostrils. The end of October had already arrived. The branches hung low with pale French pears; now, touched with crimson, the ripe fruits, blown by the wind, felt like stones before his feet.

One side of the field lay beside a narrow path, and the other side followed along the edge of a kitchen garden that belonged to a neighboring farmhouse, with its red tiled roof. He could hear the farmers walking along in their wooden clogs; on the other side, he heard the sound of a hoe digging in the garden; and all the while he walked, smelling the odors of the freshly ripened fruit. It was as though he could absorb into his body the very life of these ripening trees.

The autumn in the *haute Seine* brought to life a new, a softer spirit in Kishimoto. His love of life, dead all these many months, suddenly came back to him. And with the birth of this new spirit, it was as though he could suddenly face again all the sin that had been living for so long inside him.[17]

Kishimoto can now return to Paris, and ultimately to Japan, with a sense of renewal; and what he comes to identify as a movement toward his own salvation now permits him to turn to his niece and attempt to move her along the same trajectory. His moment of truth produces a double movement.

A New Life thus chronicles Tōson's response to his trip on an emotional level. Yet even in such an emotional and introspective work of fiction, Tōson's artistic responses, and surely on some level certain unconscious aspects of his most personal emotional responses as well, were colored by literary models he had absorbed previously, or assimilated during his visit to France. A look at all three of the books that he wrote identifies these models, and Tōson's reactions to them, quite clearly.

The first of them was specifically French, the story of Abelard and Heloise. Tōson mentions these two doomed twelfth-century lovers again and again, and in *A New Life* they assume an almost archetypal status. Tōson mentions his reading of the François Villon "Ballad of Dead Ladies," in the famous translation by Dante Gabriel Rossetti, and how much he had been moved by the sections on the pair.

> Where's Heloise, the learned nun,
>> For whose sake Abeillard, I ween,
> Lost manhood and put priesthood on?
>> (From Love he won such dule and teen!)
>> And where, I pray you, is the Queen
> Who willed that Buridan should steer
>> Sewed in a sack's mouth down the Seine . . .
> But where are the snows of yester-year?

Tōson transfers to Kishimoto his attraction to the poem and to the legend; in a striking scene, Kishimoto leads a Japanese colleague to the Père Lachaise cemetery to see the graves of the doomed lovers.

> We finally found ourselves standing before an old pavilion. Inside were the graves of Heloise and Abelard. The statues of the two, in a sleeping position, were resting there. And their names were carved on the mossy stone. When we went closer, it looked like a lovers' double grave, yet such was not the case. How surprising it was to see both figures, sleeping, laid out with their pillows side by side. One of my friends said, "Just what you might expect—France is really the country of love!" Yet only in a Catholic country might one find such an old-fashioned tomb as this. Many have visited the site. And many men and women have cut their names on the metal fence surrounding the tomb. When it comes to such things, Japan and the West are the same. Everyone, everywhere, would like to resemble those two.[18]

Later, Kishimoto reflects again on the lovers.

> He thought of them . . . sleeping together in the old, blackened tomb. The two served as a symbol of the world of profound rapture. They represented the very shape of the unfathomable trust between man and woman. Kishimoto, unlike his friend, had not laughed at the grave. Thinking of the figures, he said to himself that the story represented a kind of fairy tale. A fairy tale, yes; but no life is as barren as life without fairy tales. And when he realized that the others did not share his enthusiasm, he came to the realization that he himself was a traveller who had walked in this same world. And when he understood this, he felt very lonely.[19]

When Kishimoto returns to Japan, he tells his niece the story of the two lovers. After she hears the story there is a pause, and she responds gravely, in deceptively simple words.

"I see. Those who are not faithful to death are quickly brought to destruction. Those who can maintain themselves for so long, like those two . . . that is a wonderful thing, isn't it?"[20]

This profound response begins the second cycle of the book, the regeneration and rebirth of the spiritual health of Kishimoto's niece. The French literary model has proved universal.

Tōson's second literary model is not a Frenchman but a Japanese, and a man less known to Western historians than he might be. Kurimoto Joun (1822–1897), a retainer to the shogun, was in fact in France when the shogunate collapsed and Emperor Meiji took over the reins of power in 1868. Kurimoto wrote down his shrewd and often surprisingly disinterested responses to life in France during his stay in Paris; Tōson, reading these documents in the same city half a century later, was struck by the penetrating intellectual and moral fortitude of his predecessor, and he thus felt a legacy from an older Japan which he perceived could help him maintain his own sense of spiritual mission and his own self-respect. In this sense, Tōson's attitudes might be said to resemble those of Mori Ōgai, who, as he did his own historical research into certain figures of the late Tokugawa period, notably the doctor Shibue Chūsai, came to forge his own strong psychological links to that earlier time. In both men the power of historical imagination produced a freshening of artistic creativity. Ōgai himself produced a number of historical works dealing with the Tokugawa period, while Tōson went on to write his masterpiece *Yoakemae* (Before the Dawn), which deals with the coming of the Meiji Restoration to a country official's family modelled to a great extent on his own. It seems clear that, without the stimulus of the trip to France and without his sense of being both a stranger and a Japanese, Tōson might never have undertaken the composition of his great novel.

Tōson's third literary point of reference, and perhaps his most important one, is more unusual still, for it was the *haiku* poet Matsuo Bashō. Tōson read a great deal of Bashō during his visit to France, and the spirit of that archetypal wanderer pervades the tonality of the entire voyage. Here are a few random samplings of Tōson's references to Bashō during Tōson's years in France.

Evening came, evening . . . when I thought to go into the streets and mix with humanity, coming and going. I stopped and sat down at a cafe. A vision came to me of Bashō, a man who passed his whole life as a vagabond. And I suddenly came to realize that I must pursue the vocation of my trip with all the vigor possible.[21]

I began my voyage with the works of Bashō in my suitcase. In my rooms here, I have found in reading *The Narrow Road to the Deep North* a surprising strength and suggestiveness, and not only because of Bashō's complexity of language. I found I could make a comparison between his experiences and my own. Bashō's works are imbued with a profound sense of transience; there is in them a sense of dwelling in unreality. And from this atmosphere in turn comes a sadness, and a manifestation of the sense of the devout. Were my feelings of transience, while I lived in Tokyo, manifested to the bustling world in such a way?[22]

I often went to the window of my room, with my book of Bashō in my hand, and in this spot, cool and breezy in the summer, I would read. The stone buildings of the Porte Royale sent in sudden sensations of heat, and I sensed always that the nights were short.

Sitting alone at my window, I murmured again and again that *haiku* of Bashō:

> The moon is in the sky
> Yet it is as though someone were absent—
> Summer at Suma beach.

. . . In it, I tasted the hardship of living as a traveller, and I felt the profound emptiness contained in that little poem.[23]

Bashō thus came to serve as the most evocative and personal of the role models adopted by Tōson on his trip, providing him with a path to artistic insight, spiritual comfort, and a glimmer of meaning concerning the process of voyage, of pilgrimage, through which Tōson was moving himself. It was through Bashō that Tōson came to realize that his trip to France held the possibility of spiritual growth, that a voyage had indeed the potential to become a pilgrimage, psychologically speaking, even if the setting were artistic and secular rather than specifically religious. And indeed, Tōson's own commitment to a kind of transcendental aesthetic is, transposed, not so distant from those commitments of Bashō, as described at the beginning of this essay. Bashō's empathy, his seeking of the roots of art in his immediate surroundings, now finds a reflection in Tōson's casting of *A New Life* in the form of a personal confession, in which virtually all the text reflects the interior responses to an immediate environment as called up in the memory of the narrator, Kishimoto, and explicated in the first person. Allowing for the differences in personal temperament and style of the two authors, and for the changed literary expectations on the part of readers, there are a number of striking resemblances in the artistic strategies employed by both men in constructing a literary narrative from their own lived experience.

Bashō's own sense of yearning, of *akogare,* for something beyond the confines of ordinary life and which found its reflection in travel is mirrored in Tōson's sense of alienation from his own culture and from his own sullied sense of self. The climate of the age in which the two writers lived, of course, was profoundly different. There is little of Bashō's personal life, in the ordinary social sense, and certainly nothing of his sexual life revealed in his travel diaries; and because of the way in which the poet has constructed his narrative of self-discovery, the questions never arise in a reader's mind, since Bashō has placed his diaries on a level of poetic discourse where such matters are not considered. In Tōson's time, however, the genres had become blurred: showing a depth of sincerity now required personal confession in realms that, until the coming of the influences of the Western novel to Japan at the end of the nineteenth century, had never properly been considered the province of high art, but rather of entertainment. There are no immortal souls in Saikaku.

Lastly, Bashō's China has been replaced by Tōson's France. A reader of Tōson's books on France, however, will pick up the continuance of a peculiar resemblance in the attitude of the two writers, despite the difference in their personal situations. Bashō, after all, was never able to see China, but could only imagine it; thus his citing of Chinese poetic models and geographical examples combines with his attitudes of yearning for something outside of his own realm of immediate understanding to create a special poignancy. By the twentieth century, however, it had become possible to visit the land of one's dreams, and this is precisely what Tōson did. Yet even during his stay, when he was in physical contact with this land of culture he wished to investigate, he still maintained a yearning for a France that he could not precisely locate, a country of the heart that did not yield itself up to mere geography. It is perhaps this quality, more than any other, which makes it possible to suggest that Tōson was on a pilgrimage rather than a tour, and that the end of that pilgrimage was personal renewal and a heightened sense of self. France therefore became the means to an end. The sense of loneliness Tōson felt, and the sense of profound beauty and sadness around him, so akin to that traditional literary virtue of *aware,* were provided him by the dislocation of his voyage. What he sought was a basis to re-create and to make whole emotions that he had felt before his departure.

Victor Turner's model for a pilgrimage seems to me to be helpful in tracing the path, psychologically speaking, that Tōson followed.[24] In Turner's paradigm the pilgrim leaves the specific social structure with which he is familiar, achieves by various kinds of displacement a "liminal experience" that provides him with a perception of larger truths, then is reintegrated into his society. Specifically, the three conditions that Turner cites as necessary for a genuine spiritual experience would seem to be met by Tōson's own witness, as expressed in his writings concerning the trip to France.

The first of these involves the pilgrim's own attitude about his role on the trip. A pilgrim sees himself as an actor, performing a rite; and he must feel estranged from his ordinary sense of self. Tōson's description of Kishimoto's first morning in France reveals a number of these characteristics in an artless but striking way.

At the door of the church a young nun walked close to Kishimoto. She held out what seemed to him, having come all the way from the other side of the globe, a kind of utensil into which contributions might be solicited. She was French. There was a beggar, sitting on the church steps. He too was French. Kishimoto climbed up higher to a stone ledge. In a corner sat an old woman selling rosaries made from wooden beads, white and purple, that would no doubt delight the country girls who came there. And this old woman was French too. Kishimoto entered and looked up at the main ceiling of the building. Above the high stone walls were hung tablets with drawings of ships, given no doubt as offerings, prayers for good fortune by the seamen of the district. He was led by a guide back, further into the interior of the church. He was shown a golden statue of the Virgin Mary, bathed in soft light from the stained glass windows; and he saw the old, worn organ. The guide too was French. Kishimoto suddenly realized that he was totally among strangers.[25]

The sense of strangeness, of being out of one's own skin, as it were, is simply but effectively conveyed; and the fact that Kishimoto had his first sense of acting out an unfamiliar scenario in a church helps underline the potential spiritual dimensions of the quest that is to follow.

Turner's second condition for a genuine pilgrimage experience involves a displacement of site; the pilgrim must give up his or her usual surroundings and travel to an unfamiliar spot, most often in the country, away from the distractions and cross-purposes of an urban environment. Kishimoto's pilgrimage has its early stages in Paris, where he comes to realize the depth of his own distance from Japan, but he achieves a sense of peace and renewal in the country-side, in the passage quoted above, when he walks among the pear trees in the countryside.

For Turner, a true pilgrim must experience his sense of a larger purpose to life on an occasion when he can feel the passage of a "symbolic time," when events seem measured not by the clock but by their importance, a time in which the most seemingly insignificant event can reveal an emotional nuance of signal importance to the pilgrim. It would seem to me that, insofar as a literary text, which must be consciously constructed, can reflect a natural mental state, Tōson's re-creation in Kishimoto of his own rebirth and conversion during his wanderings in the *haute Seine* as described in the same passage reveals quite well the symbolic weight of every moment, in which the simplest things of nature—the fruit, the roofs of the houses, the wind—seem to loom as powerful emotional archetypes in his own spiritual landscape, so that walking through them takes on a significance that goes far beyond the time involved. And if, as Turner maintains, the "liminal experience" of the pilgrim allows him to gain a sense of peace with himself, of being one with all in *communitas,* in a state that, in Turner's words, "releases the pilgrim from role playing and its guilts," then Tōson, in his guise as Kishimoto, is accurate in using the word "reborn" to describe his own spiritual state. In this sense, Tōson remains close to Bashō, who maintained that "what is important is to keep our mind high in the world of true understand-ing, and returning to the world of our daily experience to seek therein the truth of beauty."

If Tōson can be placed in the long line of Japanese artistic pilgrims seeking grace and understanding through this particular line of displacement, then, it might be asked in conclusion, to what extent was Tōson exceptional? Or, to put the question in another way, what did the experience of France contribute to his growth as a writer, an artist, a human being? France and French culture certainly did contribute something to the growth of his intellectual and artistic understanding, as his writings indicate. By the same token, however, these same writings make clear that France was a means, not an end, the way by which rebirth and a sense of renewal might be achieved. What is more, France and French culture seemed a uniquely effective environment to foster such a means, not only for Tōson but for dozens of painters, poets, novelists, and intellectuals since before the turn of the century. Why should this be? Some would analyze the importance of France in terms of influences absorbed, the number of books translated, French painters taken on as teachers, and so forth. I would hazard a guess, however, that, if Tōson can serve as a useful model of the French experience for the modern Japanese, as he certainly did, then the narrow question of influences ultimately has comparatively little to do with the insights gained, and the artistic successes achieved, by the best of the Japanese who travelled to Paris and elsewhere. Rather, France, perhaps uniquely among other countries in the world, was able to provide in and of itself the kind of cultural setting, and the kind of cultural assumptions, that could permit the hope of pilgrimage and renewal for these Japanese writers and artists. As the process was one in which an artist searched to find the means to come to terms with himself, French poetry, painting, and ideas might provide the means by which this happened; but more important, it seems to me, was the fact that France provided an environment in which art, the pilgrimage of art, was itself a respected venture. Tōson grew as a writer and a man less because of the intellectual stimulus gained from his exposure to the newest currents in French artistic and intellectual life (although he enjoyed and profited from these exchanges) than from a heightened sense of himself gained from reading a writer like Bashō. Indeed, his accommodation to Western art had considerable limits; yet only the French experience could allow him to compose his novel of rebirth.

French society provided three conditions, all of them crucial to Tōson and his contemporaries. Most important of them was a confidence, shared among artists, intelligentsia, and the general educated public, in the importance of the arts; and unlike the self-conscious and sometimes self-serving attitudes toward the arts prevalent in this country, the simple assumption of the centrality of the arts to culture in France, a conviction that needed no justification, went far to making Paris the capital of the arts, attracting not only the Japanese, but Americans, British, Romanians, Spaniards, Indonesians, indeed all who were interested in the arts and wanted to participate in their creation. Allied to this was an implicit democracy; the traditions of the arts, and the possibility of success in mastering them, were open to all. Artists, writers, and composers working in Paris were not alone in their ability to recognize and champion creative work of high merit, whatever its origins; French audiences were able to do the same. Fujita Tsuguji might sell his paintings, Gershwin might study with Ravel, Bakst might produce his superb ballet stage designs, all in Paris. Allied to this as well was a third assumption, that of the avant-garde; Paris was a place to come to renew and then create, not merely to follow older traditions. A painter no longer needed to be steeped in the traditions of French art from Poussin to Ingres and Delacroix in order to reach high achievement; a poet might draw on Hugo, Verlaine, and Mallarmé, but the new works could be as different as those of an Aragon or a Rilke.

Many Japanese writers, artists, and painters were able to plunge themselves into this heady milieu. Some had difficulties, particularly because they felt they had so much to learn that they could not go beyond the status quo in order to participate in the milieu of an avant-garde that could in turn offer them the possibility of real success in European terms. Some succeeded brilliantly at infusing new ideas into the realm of Japanese arts and ideas. One needs only to think of the philosopher and aesthetician Kuki Shūzō (1888–1941), who was in Germany, then France from 1922 to 1929, and who returned to Japan to introduce contemporary European philosophy, including an early version of existentialism, and write such influential and still stimulating works as *Iki no kōzō* (The Structure of the Chic), an extraordinary evocation of the arts of the Tokugawa period. There is as well the example of the poet Nishiwaki Junzaburō (1894–1982), a friend of Pound and Eliot, who wrote poetry in French and English, a "beggar for Europe" by his own confession, who returned to Japan to introduce surrealism, compose a superb body of modernist verse, and translate Eliot's *Four Quartets*. And a dozen others. The impact of France on the evolution of Japanese artistic and intellectual life between the wars was certainly as powerful as that brought about in the United States by the arrival of so many Europeans escaping the growth of Hitlerism in Germany; one difference might be the fact that Americans tended to receive passively the arrival of the Brechts, Stravinskys, Adornos, and Lévi-Strausses, while Japanese intellectuals and artists were always willing to go to France, if they could, to actively seek out their mentors. The best of these "travellers from an antique land" succeeded in their own spiritual voyages because, like Shelley's traveller, they believed that art in the largest sense was the only force beyond decay in their cultural and often personal lives, and because they were intent, like Tōson, on maintaining their own integrity while they learned to interpret and reinterpret what they already understood in terms of something European they had come to admire. That special integrity, of course, bears a close and moving resemblance to *makoto,* the ancient virtue of sincerity, that has always played such a crucial role in Japanese art, and in Japanese life. The convictions of those travellers were thus reinforced by their French experience, and the best of the work they created pays homage both to their place of origin and those regions through which they journeyed in search of themselves.

2

Three Japanese Painters in Paris
The Interwar Years

INTELLECTUAL historians often select diverse materials for their investigations into the attitudes, assumptions, and philosophical commitments of a particular historical epoch. In charting the movements, obsessions, and enthusiasms of various periods in European history since the Renaissance, for example, such cultural historians as Arnold Hauser and E. H. Gombrich have made stimulating use of chosen examples in painting, architecture, and sculpture to provide visual evidence of the process by which Europeans have conceptualized their relations with their physical and spiritual world. The ideas and concepts that emerge from an examination of the visual arts are usually found, in turn, to have wider application in helping to assess the shifting nature of more general sensibilities in societies as they change. Such a method has long been an accepted part of European studies, but in the field of Japanese history we have yet to make much systematic use of a correspondingly rich store of material. True, the traditional arts up until the end of the Tokugawa period have been used by such writers as Langdon Warner as symbols of larger cultural attitudes; then too, the accomplishments of contemporary Japanese art are often cited as representative of wider currents in modern Japanese life, especially when those currents parallel our own. But surprisingly, little attention has been paid to that provocative period from about 1905 through the early 1930s, when so many movements were launched in the visual arts.

Before the end of the first decade of the century, two generations of Japanese artists had already mastered the techniques of Western oil painting and had managed to stimulate in the Japanese public an ability to appreciate to a significant extent the ideals and philosophic background of late-nineteenth-century European art. By 1910 a number of important Japanese painters had begun serious study in Europe and were able, on returning to Japan, to make viable careers for themselves, teaching, producing paintings for private collectors, and, on occasion, persuading museums and other public institutions to buy their work and help sustain them in their careers. Painting in the Western style had become an accepted and acceptable part of Japanese artistic life, and one that was considered to be of genuine importance in the general Japanese cultural and intellectual world.

Despite the importance of these efforts, however, Western scholars of modern Japan have given little attention to the details of what these artists felt themselves attempting to achieve; nor has much effort been made to evaluate the larger significance of the accomplishments of the period. Why should this be so? One reason may be that, since so much importance is given, in this country at least, to connoisseurship in the study of the visual arts, those who study the works produced by Japanese during this period may feel that these painters have not reached the highest level. True, there is doubtless no Japanese Matisse, no Japanese Vlaminck. What is more, I suspect that even if there were Japanese artists of that supreme quality, a further prejudice might arise, indicating that there could not *be* a Japanese Matisse. Matisse is French; and although his strength is uniquely his own, he grows out of the heritage of French art created in the previous century. Thus a Japanese who paints in a style approximating the canons of modern European art would by definition fail to be of the first rank; his work, while contemporary in spirit, would still appear derivative.

I would argue, however, that at least in terms of cultural and intellectual history the real contribution of these Japanese artists does not lie in such absolute terms. Rather, their worth might be better judged in terms of the significance, culturally speaking, of what they and their contemporaries felt they were trying to accomplish. As I am not an art historian, it is simpler for me to shift the focus of judgement, and perhaps I am attempting to move it too far. Still, I believe the lives and works of these men can most profitably be studied in terms of the way in which they illustrate and suggest the best of what their culture was trying to achieve during the period. From a contemporary point of view, Japan has put herself altogether in the international world of art. The processes she underwent in the interwar period represent crucial, indeed inevitable steps that have brought about a present stage of accomplishment. From this perspective the work that artists created in the earlier years of the century takes on a real and continuing significance. The painting of the best of these artists shows great skill, and their dedication to the values and ideals of European, or perhaps I should say, of world art, is touching, often heroic. From the point of view of cultural history, then, such men claim our attention.

Courage was certainly involved in the attempt made by these painters to grasp, understand, and embrace a culture so different from their own. By this period Japan possessed a significant number of intellectuals who wanted to measure their ideas and their work against international, not national standards. In the arts that standard meant Europe. Takamura Kōtarō (1883–1956), the poet and sculptor, for example, captured beautifully the atmosphere of excitement and fulfillment that Europe provided for the Japanese of this period in a number of poems written during his stay in France. A brief sample will convey the level of emotional energy stimulated. This particular poem, of which only a brief fragment is reproduced here, was published in 1921, and probably first drafted in 1908.

Cathedral in the Thrashing Rain

O another deluge of wind and rain.
Collar turned up, getting drenched in this splashing rain,
and looking up at you—it's me,
me who never fails to come here once a day.
It's that Japanese.
This morning
about daybreak the storm suddenly went violent, terrible
and now is blowing through Paris from one end to the other.
I have yet to know the directions of this land.
I don't even know which way this storm is facing, raging over Ile-de-
    France.
Only because even today I wanted to stand here
and look up at you, Cathedral of Notre-Dame de Paris,
I came, getting drenched,
only because I wanted to touch you,
only because I wanted to kiss your skin, the stone, unknown to anyone.
(tr. Hiroaki Sato)[1]

On his return to Japan, Kōtarō put forth a credo of individualism that summed up the new spirit felt by many of his contemporaries. His powerful statements, often published in the small intellectual magazines of the day, represented an attitude at the opposite extreme from those traditional ideas concerning the role of the artist that had continued to guide many artistic circles even after the end of the Tokugawa period. One particularly striking essay, entitled "The Green Sun," dates from 1910, in which he wrote:

> I desire absolute freedom of art. Consequently, I recognize the limit-less authority of the individuality of the artist. I would like to make my starting point the evaluation of this individuality. I would like to study individuality itself and not question its existence. If another man sees an object I believe is green but that he says is red, I would like to evaluate the manner in which he handles the red object—based on the assumption that the object is indeed red. I do not want to question his belief that the object is red. Rather, I welcome him because his conception of nature differs from mine. I want to know to what degree he has captured the truth of nature; I also want to know the depth and richness of his emotions. Even if two or three artists should paint a "green sun," I would never criticize them, for I myself may see a "green sun" at some point. [2]

It was in such an atmosphere that the artists of the interwar generations began their work. For them, the assumptions made by Kōtarō were new, complex, and demanded special self-expectations. Not everyone could meet them, but the struggle itself was felt to be exhilarating.

In this context, I would like to examine briefly the careers of three painters who went to Paris in the period, three who took on Europe whole. Their varied responses to their sense of artistic vocation show the problems and the accomplishments of the whole period in a special light, and one that can help us formulate larger considerations about the development of modern Japanese culture in general.

Before looking at the lives and work of these three painters, however, there are several related points that should be made so as to suggest some of the difficulties and restraints that limited and shaped their work. To some extent the artists were aware themselves of these problems; to a degree, however, an awareness of these difficulties has only arisen later, by historical hindsight.

The first concerns the issue of copying versus creativity. Traditionally, in Europe and Japan alike, young artists copied and worked under a master in his studio until they learned the essentials of their craft. Such a process was a perfectly natural part of becoming a competent artist. Now, young Japanese, wanting to learn to paint in the European fashion, were anxious to find the means to learn the requisite skills. Therefore they copied Western painters just as they might have copied their own seniors before the end of the nineteenth century. By the early years of this century, however, there was no longer any universally accepted style in Western painting. Copying no longer put an artist into the mainstream of accepted technique. It relegated him to a secondary place, ranked him with those who could show no individuality. The problem was the same, in one sense, for Western artists, but at least they were familiar with the general idiom. The Japanese still had to master it.

Secondly, by the early years of the century, the ideas of art in the West were changing so fast that no accepted canons of taste could universally be put forth. In one sense there were as many kinds of Western "art" as there were first-rate painters. Such a situation was quite new. Coming to France to find the fount of Western art, the Japanese found that what they had thought to constitute those fundamental assumptions were in danger of disappearing.

In the third place, it seems to me that, in almost all cases, the successful activities of an "avant-garde" in any culture require—how shall I put it?—a "garde," a genuine tradition against which to react. Japanese painters arriving in Europe saw Impressionists reacting against the Salon, then Cubists reacting against the Impressionists, then Surrealists superseding Cubists. All of these rapidly changing styles were created in reaction to what had come before. Yet the Japanese artists, not having participated in the previous movements, found it difficult to grasp the real purposes of any particular style. In a sense an accident of history made them enter into a dialogue without an adequate opportunity, as it were, to know the original subject of conversation. The fact that contemporary Japanese art has now seen some success surely has a good deal to do with the fact that postwar Japanese artists can genuinely engage in a dialogue with a previous Japanese generation, and so establish themselves and their point of view on the basis of assumptions that have already taken root in their own culture. In 1910, even in 1920 and after, Japanese painters working in advanced styles found themselves working in a void, and this emptiness was often dangerous to them spiritually as well as artistically.

Of course, not all the painters in this period felt such difficulties. Basically there seem to have been three general responses by Japanese painters to the European stimulus. One was to attempt to assimilate European ideas and to become one with them. A second was to try to find one's way while maintaining an alien integrity. A third was to synthesize the two through skill and suppleness of spirit. I have chosen an example from each category.

The first was the greatest assimilator of all, Fujita Tsuguji (1886–1968). Fujita saw Western art as an opportunity, and one that he wished to take. Indeed, he died a Catholic and a French citizen, changing his name first to Tsugouharu Foujita, then to Léonard Foujita. Fujita was a fine painter and is still so regarded; his works continue to command high prices, and several of his works hang in the Museum of Modern Art at the Centre Beaubourg in Paris. Yet there is still some feeling, at least in Japan, that he took the opportunities too easily and promoted himself too assiduously. "Ah," he is reported to have remarked to one of his friends, "Will I be forgiven for my lack of fidelity?" Yet "fidelity" to what? An answer to that question would do much to explain the cultural assumptions of the Japanese during the interwar period.

Fujita's father was a wealthy doctor, of powerful personality, who found himself persuaded to allow his son to enter the arts. Fujita was graduated from the Tokyo School of Fine Arts in 1910, and went off to Paris at age 27 in 1913. Fujita took to the trappings of French artistic life at once and soon became a fixture at La Rotonde, the Montparnasse cafe frequented by so many of the important artistic figures of the period. He found himself, by his own confession, totally unprepared for the art he found in Paris. All the Western traditions he had so painstakingly studied in Tokyo had been superseded. Fujita's prior conception of contemporary Western art had been a mild form of Impressionism; now he found himself faced with Cubism at a time when, as he wrote, "I didn't even know of the existence of Cézanne." After a series of struggles, both artistic and financial, he found his way by 1918 and began to sell a certain amount of his work with success. Part of that success involved his first marriage: Fernande Vallé was at the time an important art dealer, and she helped guide his taste and talent. By 1920 he had developed his "trademark," paintings elegant in design, often of women whose flesh was painted as an undulating surface on which a black outline was superimposed, providing a combination of linear clarity and sensuous space unusual in French art at the time. Fujita had managed in a small way to become original within the contemporary canon of possibilities.

Japanese critics have pointed out that Fujita's style enabled him to use and reproduce the visual world yet break through the banality of photographic "truth" in order to achieve his own means of self-expression. Fujita insisted that an artist must not copy; on the other hand, he must use the techniques that he understands best. At a later point Fujita expressed in an interview the opinion that the Japanese could make better use of black and white than European artists because of a long tradition of ink painting and woodblock print design. Line, and outline, were a part of the national heritage of artistic skill. In some ways Fujita's work is a highly successful juxtaposition of Eastern technique with Western medium and subject matter. The result is pleasing, flattering—and genuinely so—to both traditions.

Fujita pointed out as well that he wanted to be an artist in the world. He was a Japanese in Paris, just as Picasso was a Spaniard in Paris. Both could partake of, benefit from, the same stimulation, he insisted. In one sense, of course, Fujita did lead quite a cosmopolitan life. Fernande was replaced by his second wife, a stunning French-woman he named "Youki," who, after she left him, became involved with the well-known French poet Robert Desnos. Fujita made a trip to Japan in 1929, to see his father, but he had more or less become a European until the late 1930s, when, for a number of reasons, some of them still obscure, Fujita threw over his European connections and returned to Japan, where he spent much of the war painting pictures of military battles for the Japanese government. The few of these battle paintings I have been able to see in reproduction are on the whole strikingly well done and certainly not patriotic in any vulgar way; still, many Japanese critics who write on the career of Fujita find the self-confessed "discipline" that he said had led him to create such works to represent merely another facet of the opportunism that allowed him to assimilate himself into the French artistic world so smoothly twenty years before.

In 1950 Fujita returned to France, this time with a Japanese wife, a simple but dedicated woman brought up in a fishing village. By 1955 he had become a French citizen, and in 1959 he converted to Catholicism. In the 1960s he took on the final major task of his long career, the creation of a series of murals for a chapel at Reims. The assimilation was complete. Or so it seemed. For many Japanese who knew of him, however, that assimilation indicated to them that Fujita actually showed little depth of conviction in his own artistic personality. In such a view, a skill in grasping the style of his time made him a fashionable painter, but could not sustain him until the end. Japanese historians of art have been particularly severe in their attitudes toward the Christian paintings done at the end of Fujita's life. From the reproductions available to me, there does seem room for a genuine doubt that he was able to bring a necessary depth of feeling to the subject matter he chose to portray. On the other hand, it might be argued, few have succeeded in this century in giving depth and profundity to overtly religious subject matter. One exception is surely Rouault, but his work often accomplishes its purposes by expressionistic techniques not a part of Fujita's delicate artistic vocabulary. Making any sort of final judgement on Fujita as a man or as an artist would require more documentation than is presently available. It is clear, however, that the attitude of those in Japan who are attempting to construct their own cultural history of this century involves an implicit assumption that worldly success, even in Paris, does not grant accomplishment; it would seem that sincerity and suffering are required as well.

My second example is that of a painter who, almost unknown when he died, has become a legend in postwar Japan and is often now regarded as perhaps the greatest spirit of all those who worked in France during the interwar years. Saeki Yūzō (1898–1928) also came to live in France and died there, by his own hand. He saw the necessary struggle for accomplishment in a very different light than Fujita, and he lived out his own personal tensions to the end. Japanese critics and art lovers, sensing that struggle, award him pride of place not only for his accomplishments, which are genuine, but for the spirit in which he brought them about. Compared with the sincerity of Saeki, Fujita seems a mere schemer.

Saeki was born in Osaka and took a strong interest in Western culture, learning the violin as a child and studying how to sketch using

European techniques. By the time he decided, at twenty, to go to Tokyo to study painting, a form of Western academicism consisting of a judicious mixture of Renoir and Cézanne was beginning to be taught in the Japanese art schools. This romantic, turn-of-the-century style represented for Saeki the sum of the techniques of European art. Four years later, when he was twenty-six, he decided that he should go to France to study painting with the teachers available there; he took all his worldly possessions and managed to convert them into enough money to finance the trip. At this point in his career Saeki had already shown real talent in the kind of academic painting in which he had been trained, and when he arrived in Paris his work was appreciated by other Japanese artists working there. After he had painted a certain number of canvases, while living on the Left Bank near the place St. Michel, a colleague managed to arrange an introduction for him to meet Maurice Vlaminck, another painter who began as a violinist and whose own spiritual journey had led him from Fauvism, early in the century, into a Cubist phase. Vlaminck looked over Saeki's work and told him that it was altogether too academic, warning him that if he wished to become a really great painter, he would have to develop his own unique personal style.

This brief encounter constituted the crucial moment in Saeki's career. He was convinced that Vlaminck's words had destroyed his whole artistic life up until that point; by the same token, he felt they had given him hope of another artistic life to come. From a larger perspective, Vlaminck's random remark suggested in a few words all the difficulties and ambiguities that had to be faced by Japanese painters of Saeki's generation.

Saeki therefore decided to stop all his academic painting exercises. He left the atelier where he was working and locked himself up in his tiny apartment to search out a personal vision. The search also took him into the countryside; he was particularly drawn to Normandy, where he painted directly from nature. He also began to paint a number of cityscapes, many of them in the poorer districts of Paris. Those paintings, while of recognizable places, seem, through the distortion of line and the simplification of color and shape, to focus rather on the artist's own interior world; the scenes portrayed in the paintings appear to reduce themselves to a kind of personal code that objectifies an inner alienation and withdrawal growing from the core of the artist's personality. Saeki's search led him closer to a sense of himself, and that sense of self in turn risked transformation into a sense of the void. By now his funds were low, he had no clients for his ever more peculiar pictures, and many of his canvases were ill prepared and already deteriorating. He could afford neither the proper grade of canvas nor of paint and sizing.

Saeki's first success came in 1925, when some of his pictures were entered in the autumn Salon, a suitable place for new painters to debut in Paris. In 1926 his brother came to visit, having assembled enough funds to take Saeki on a trip to Italy then back to Japan.

Buoyed by the beginnings of success in Paris, Saeki opened a studio in Tokyo, only to confront a new problem. His struggle for a personal vision had now pushed him beyond the limits of understanding of the Japanese public, which still retained a Renoir-like image of Western art that by now represented in Europe only the blandest academicism. Early reviewers of his Japanese exhibit criticized his work as "too brutal," or "a copy of Utrillo." The Japanese public seemed incapable of seeing what Saeki had added of his own to this new rhetoric he had brought back from Paris. Saeki also painted a certain number of works in Japan; these are his least successful pictures and seem to illustrate a wildness and uncertainty of artistic direction. They suggest the need for a fantasy of escape.

Without acceptance in his own culture, Saeki decided to go back to France in 1927. Somehow he found the funds to take his wife and young child along. They rented an inexpensive apartment in the Montparnasse district; the rooms were badly heated, and Saeki's health began to deteriorate. Nevertheless his work improved. He began to regain confidence in himself, and offers to buy his canvases came from potential French patrons. He threw himself into a frenzy of work, going out to paint in the streets of Paris in all weathers. His haunted, empty cafes and strange cluttered billboards, all rendered in a nervous, restless line, represent a remarkable artistic statement, capturing both his own loneliness and the emptiness he found around him. Saeki was indeed on the edge of finding a unique vision, but the cost was too great. One evening he put down his brush and said to his wife, "My work is finished." He seemed terrified of death, and she, frightened for him, tried to seek help. He made one suicide attempt, then, two weeks later, succeeded in killing himself. His wife took the little money she had left, packed up his work, and began the long trip home to Japan.

Of course this is not the end of the story. In 1929 a one-man show of Saeki's work was held in Tokyo, and his paintings were now greeted with enormous critical acclaim. His work was bought up, protected, and exhibited. By the postwar years, Saeki's reputation had soared to the highest level. For the Japanese, he had achieved the genuine artistic success denied him during his lifetime.

The career of Saeki contains many ironies. At his best, he certainly was a brilliant painter, perhaps the most provocative of his genera-tion, and a man whose vision continues to have genuine artistic value. In terms of cultural history, Saeki's experience, and the atten-tion he ultimately attracted among the citizens of his own country, remains significant. His whole career is a testament to the power that art can have on a gifted individual, a power so great that, in this case, the person involved could summon the bravery to overthrow not only the traditions he knew from his own culture but the very tradition that he thought he had gone to Europe to learn. In that perspective Saeki's painting becomes a record of his struggle to penetrate not only the techniques but the values of another culture, all in order to attempt to go beyond them. In those terms Saeki can surely be judged a brave man, and this is part of his enduring attraction to the Japanese public, where sincerity of purpose continues to inform, and sometimes deform, purely artistic judgements. Even if he had not been so gifted, however, Saeki's career would have considerable value as an example of the problems of competing cultures. In terms of the development of the traditions of modern art in Japan, even imperfect art can teach as much or more than a masterpiece.

Umehara Ryūzaburō (1888–1986), the third painter I have chosen to discuss, was active during those years, and long after, and is the unquestioned leader of modern Japanese painters who studied in France. During his long and productive life Umehara managed to relate East and West, blend his own personal perceptions with the appropriate canons of taste of both traditions, and achieve an artistic synthesis appropriate to both. In this endeavor he has been remark-ably successful, and his large, elegant, and satisfying canvases can be seen in most Japanese museums that include modern Japanese art in their collections. Until just a few years ago Umehara kept busy at work in his Tokyo studio, a kind of "old man, mad about Western style painting," as free spirited as at the turn of the century.

Like Fujita and Saeki, Umehara was trained in Japan in the kind of Post-Impressionist painting technique that had become the standard. He took up his formal studies in 1906; two years later, when he was twenty, he went to France with the idea of somehow meeting and studying with Renoir. He visited Renoir at his home in Cagnes in the south of France; delighted with the talents of this young Japanese painter, Renoir took him on as a student and helped him both as teacher and patron. By 1911 Umehara had met Picasso and, at his suggestion, toured Spain to see other landscapes and other light. Back in Paris in 1912, he took an apartment near Notre Dame (which figures in some of his paintings of the period) and travelled from time to time to see various sites in Italy as well. In the following year, he bid Renoir good-bye, returned to Japan by train through Russia, and arrived back in his home city of Kyoto, where he held his first exhibit.

Umehara's family had connections with the silk-weaving industry in Kyoto. The artist's childhood exposure to the great traditional methods of design, plus his work with Renoir and his interest in the Fauvists, gave him a comfortable, distinctive style that could bridge the enthusiasm of the French and Japanese publics alike. Umehara developed flat, decorative patterns, used in outline, which he filled in with brilliant, nuanced colors to provide a strong emotional effect. The harmonies he evolved bear a recognizable relationship to the object or landscape chosen as subject matter, yet serve as well to provide a juxtaposition of shades and hues satisfying for its own sake. Umehara's pictures took on the freedom of Western painting while retaining a control of color worthy of the great Japanese woodblock artists of the past.

From the beginning Umehara found success in Japan, and by the 1920s a show of his work was held in Paris as well. Umehara travelled back to France when he learned of the death of Renoir in 1919, and he spent some time visiting with the artist's family, with whom he had become quite close. On his way back to Japan he again travelled through Europe, drawing and sketching as he went.

Umehara's career continued on in a similar vein. His brilliant sense of color and pattern never deserted him, and he came to supply his skill not only to the human figure but to a wider variety of landscape possibilities. He travelled extensively in Japan and was especially impressed by the semitropical scenery in southern Kyushu; in particular, his paintings done in the Kagoshima area show that he at last found certain affinities between that scenery and the south of

SAEKI YŪZŌ (1898–1928)
Posters and the Terrace of a Cafe, 1927
Oil on canvas, 53.5 × 65 cm
Bridgestone Museum, Tokyo

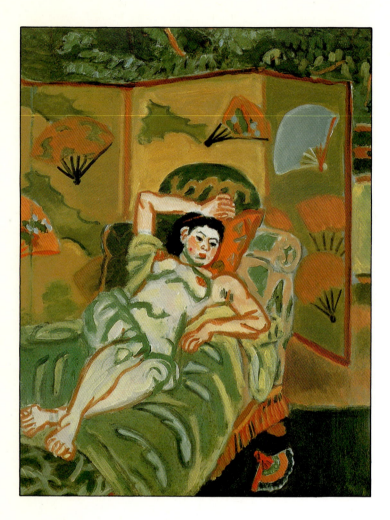

UMEHARA RYŪZABURŌ (1888–1986)
Nude with Fans, 1938
Oil on canvas, 81 × 61 cm
Ohara Museum of Art, Kurashiki

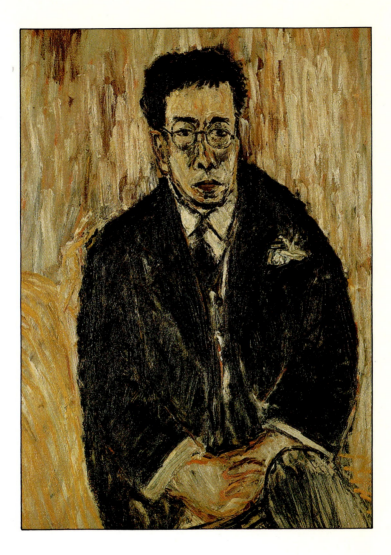

HASEGAWA TOSHIYUKI (1891–1940)
Portrait of Kishida Kunio, 1930
Oil on canvas, 74 × 54 cm
Tokyo National Museum of Modern Art

Fujita Tsuguji (Foujita Tsugouharu) (1886–1968)
Portrait of Mrs. E. C. Chadbourne, 1922
Tempera on canvas, 89.2 × 146.1 cm, Gift of
 Mrs. Emily Crane Chadborne

France. In 1939 he made a visit to China, where he painted the streets and temples of Peking with the same freshness of color that he brought to Japanese and European subjects.

After the war Umehara returned to France on a number of occasions, often with his children and grandchildren. His later, looser style seems especially appropriate to a series of scenes of Venice, with their thick surface of paint and elegant juxtapositions of color. Umehara continued to move back and forth between the two worlds of France and Japan as though he belonged naturally in both. The cultural contrasts that seemed to stand as a source of anguish for an artist like Saeki became, for Umehara, an opportunity to express his plenitude of spirit.

Each of these painters, then, when they encountered Europe, was forced to respond in a highly personal way in order to wrest creation and synthesis from two disparate cultural systems. In a real sense, the three represent the range of possible response. Fujita went over to Europe. Saeki went on alone to forge his own vision while regarding the systems as in potential conflict. Umehara was best able to synthesize elements from both and remain himself.

It is inappropriate, if not impossible, to say which of these responses may be the most satisfactory for an artist of those years; certainly the sense of tension can be felt in the work of all of these men, and indeed in the efforts of so many of the artists and intellectuals who tried to absorb the West while maintaining their own identity, their own individuality. The poet Ishikawa Takuboku (1885–1912) wrote in his 1909 diary, in a passage composed in English, a language he was making efforts to learn, of the "burning summer and the green-colored struggle." All three painters would have understood Takuboku's apprehensions.

Some would argue that, in the postwar period, a cultural synthesis has been achieved in Japan. If that is so, then the record of that struggle to achieve it, seen from the perspective of this generation, has a beauty, and a significance, in and of itself. The art of the interwar years provides an evocative means to observe both visually and intellectually the phenomenon of one culture struggling to absorb another while attempting to maintain its own integrity.

3

Kishida Kunio
Europe as Art Object

THE NATURE of Asian and Western literary and cultural relations raises relatively complex questions when it comes to modern Japan. Even a cursory examination of the problems involved suggests some wide-ranging conflicts that can bear witness in turn to larger questions related to the whole process of social and cultural development in Japan since the Meiji Restoration began in 1868. The modern theatre in Japan has been especially subject to a series of cultural shocks intimately involved with Japan's encounters with the West. Some of the most poignant of these are particularly visible in the career of Kishida Kunio (1890–1954), who lived in Paris in the early 1920s and worked with the famous Vieux Colombier troupe of Jacques Copeau. When Kishida returned to Japan, he did a great deal to bring both the artistic values and techniques of the French theatre to bear on the development of modern Japanese dramaturgy.

Or so it is said. On the other hand, it can be argued that, whatever Kishida's debt to the West might have been, it consisted of something different, and more important, than any mere imitation of literary or theatrical technique. Kishida, a remarkably reticent man, never enlarged on his own intellectual education in sufficient detail to provide any full answer as to what his European experience ultimately meant to him. Some clue, however, can be found in a short article he wrote in connection with his general observations on the modern French theatre.

Toward the end of 1922, Stanislavsky's Moscow Art Theatre visited Paris. On the evening before the opening performance, the manager of the Théâtre des Champs-Elysées gave an elaborate welcoming party

38

for the troupe in his theatre, in order to introduce them to various theatrical groups in Paris. That scene is one that I will find hard to forget for the rest of my life.

Stanislavsky was in the center; with him was Chekhov's widow and other prominent members of the troupe. Antoine, now an old man, stood nearby. He was the one who began the modern French movement with his Théâtre Libre. Near him, arms folded, stood Jacques Copeau. The seats were filled with spectators.

Antoine greeted Stanislavsky, who replied in charming, if naive French that he was very much moved by the tribute paid to him and his troupe. He then continued: "My interest in the theatre is due to the inspiration I received from my own trips to Paris. And again, if our own purpose has been to bring something new to the theatre of my country, it has been because of the influence of the pioneer of us all, Antoine."

Lastly, he said, "Some of you may feel that since we perform our plays in Russian, much of our art will be lost to you. But this fear is without foundation. For above the level of our Russian language, we convey things that any human being can understand; and we are confident that we can hold your interest."[1]

There are two points that might be noted here, in light of Kishida's own work in the modern Japanese theatre. During the course of these remarks, Stanislavsky expressed a set of ideas that must have impressed Kishida very deeply. The first concerns the debt of one artist to another; even if the artists are from different cultures, that debt is a good and a natural thing. Secondly, true art goes beyond the dictates of the language and culture of a particular country; and insofar as one can participate in the creation, or in the enjoyment, of that art, one leads a fuller life as a human being, beyond the confines of one's particular cultural context.

Kishida was extremely susceptible to both of these ideas. He went back to Japan with an artistic consciousness shaped and expanded by those years in France, and that consciousness became his particular burden to bear for the rest of his life.

In Kishida's work for the modern Japanese theatre, he certainly introduced European, often specifically French techniques to his contemporaries. But it would be a mistake, I think, to say that such represented the sum of his purposes. He did want to train stage actors and improve dialogue writing, for example, and of course he applied what he knew to the situation he found. But what he really

set out to do was to seek a means to respond with his whole personality to Europe as an art object, one that he revered. He wished to
enter into the spirit of that object so as to make use of his identification with it in his own creative work, his writing for the theatre. In
that sense, Kishida embarked on a trajectory that was to symbolize
the activity of the whole of Japanese society. In that regard he was
able to function as what A. G. Lehmann has characterized as an
"artist canary," one of a category of writers capable of using "their
intuitive powers to see patterns forming that the common run of their
contemporaries have not yet detected . . . with highly sensitive
antennae, able to pick up signals not yet audible to ordinary receiv-
ers . . . that might be compared with canaries that miners used to
take down shafts with them to give early warning of toxic gases . . ."[2]

When Kishida returned to Japan in 1923, he was to play a double
role, first as a man, distanced from his particular culture by his own
self-consciousness, and then only secondly as a Japanese. At first the
double role was a relatively pleasant one to play, for there were few
conflicts between the two. The "new spirit" he introduced into the
modern Japanese theatre was much appreciated by his contemporaries, and the lyrical humor of his writing seemed fresh and thus, to his
readers and spectators, somehow French inspired. I would like to
suggest, however, that what he wrote owed more to his ability to
observe his surroundings with objective detachment than to anything
specifically French. Take, for example, a scene from his very popular
play *Kami fūsen* (Paper Balloon), written in 1925. This short sketch
chronicles the attitudes of a young husband and wife who are learning to adjust to each other and to the realities of married life. She
decides to go off by herself on a Sunday to assert her independence.

HUSBAND.   . . . well then, I suppose that it is all right with me. But if
           you're not there, what will I do about lunch?
WIFE.   I've made a few simple preparations for you.
HUSBAND.   And in the evening?
WIFE.   When I go out I'll stop by the corner restaurant and have
           them deliver some eggs and rice to you.
HUSBAND.   Again? And I suppose you'll be late coming home.
WIFE.   That's a good question. I really don't know, but if it gets
           past ten o'clock, go ahead and fix your bed and go to
           sleep.

HUSBAND.   Do you have any money?
WIFE.   Not a penny.
HUSBAND.   Well, let me give you this. Here's ten yen.
WIFE.   Thanks.
HUSBAND.   The night wind is cold now, so don't forget to take a muffler.
WIFE.   Sure.
HUSBAND.   Well now, I guess I'll curl up and read a book. Just heat the water up for a bath before you go. If any guests drop by, we have some old biscuits left. I don't think I'll shave today. Ah, what a nice peaceful Sunday this is . . .
WIFE.   [*Silent, she stares at the floor.*]
HUSBAND.   Now what?
WIFE.   You're impossible!
HUSBAND.   Impossible? In what way?
WIFE.   In every way![3]

The couple's relationship is very real, and the bantering between them seems quite natural. What is special, however, is the writer's objectivity; he can draw back far enough to see the foibles of both. Some Japanese critics have called Kishida a moralist, and it is surely this objective, detached quality in his writing, this ability to make distinctions, that suggests this aspect of his mentality. Again, such detachment is less specifically French than it is modern, a manifestation of self-consciousness concerning *any* values that seems so much a hallmark of our century.

Kishida's detachment was a simpler burden to bear in the intellectual atmosphere of Japan in the 1920s than during the difficult period of the late 1930s, leading up to and including the war years. His own plays grew more skillful in construction and harsher in their observations of contemporary society. In his 1936 play, *Sawa shi no futari musume* (Mr. Sawa's Two Daughters), which represents for many Kishida's masterpiece, he came closest to autobiography, nearest to revealing the emptiness he found at the bottom of Japanese moral and spiritual life. Again, the context of Japan at that moment suggests less of any specifically French flavor than of an atmosphere, based on Kishida's objective observations, of a darkening sense of fatigue over the prospects for Japanese culture at that time.

A speech by Sawa, as he remembers an experience while a young man in France, may serve as a poetic symbol of the isolation Kishida felt was sapping the creative energies of many in his generation.

SAWA. . . . when I first entered the Foreign Office, I was sent to study French at Deauville. In the lodging house where I stayed, there were two old ladies, oh, about fifty years old or so. . . . do you know that for more than ten years, those two had never spoken? That's what I heard. Isn't that extraordinary? They had disagreed about something or other, and so they never spoke. Of course, in front of other people they maintained a perfectly normal appearance. I used to watch one following the other as the pair of them would sweep the path, right up to the gate. It was quite charming, in fact.

As I said, they never spoke, for ten years. I suppose there were some things that had to be discussed between them, though. . . . I can remember sitting in the dining room, looking at the two of them, countless times. One would occupy one side of the table, and the other would sit across on the other side and glare at her. Sometimes it made me nervous, but sometimes it struck me as really quite amusing, you know. When things really got bad, they would have a terrible quarrel.

You see, it wasn't just the fact that something had happened between them that made them angry. They *disliked* each other so much. You would think one of them would just go away. But they didn't. How interesting that foreigners seem to react this way. For them, to go away would mean to lose.[4]

The two women Sawa discusses are French, but the dangerous silence to which Kishida calls attention is redolent of the attitudes of the Japanese intelligentsia before the ascendancy of the military in the late 1930s.

Kishida, however, was by no means ready to abandon his second role, that of a Japanese, and the tensions of carrying on while maintaining this double sense of himself continued to plague him. He tried to cooperate to some extent with the wartime government (which earned him an opprobrious reputation with the postwar Marxist critics) in order to keep his theatre company, the Bungakuza, open; but by 1943 he abandoned that attempt as well and retired to the country to wait for what he thought would be the end.

Kishida's writings during that period show him wrestling with his commitments to objectivity and with his resolution to embrace neither the mindless attitudes of those who supported the war nor the fanaticism of those few who resisted it. A brief paragraph he wrote at the time may serve to reveal the state of his mind more quickly than any description that I might provide.

> I am not ashamed to be born a Japanese, nor am I proud of the fact. Indeed this fact, like the very fact of birth itself, is a question of fate. It is accidental; and no human effort can do anything to change it. Thus I feel no compunction to complain. And I have no reason to feel any special thanks. Such must always be my premise.[5]

There is only cold comfort, perhaps, in these words, yet Kishida attempted to remain true to the objectivity gained from his European experience.

Whether Kishida is a great Japanese writer is a question that does not bear directly on my remarks here. At the least, he was a very gifted one, and his time in France had, at the deepest level, given him the conviction that to try to be a human being, in the fullest sense of the word, involved a search that was more important in itself than any need to embrace a preconceived set of ideas and values, Japanese or otherwise. Such convictions made Kishida a lonely man, and a thoroughly modern one.

Ultimately the study of the meaning of Europe on the work of Kishida, and others like him, must embrace not only an analysis of the adaption of certain literary techniques—and in his case, such a study would reveal that he made such adaptions as a matter of common sense to improve the young modern Japanese theatre at the time —but of the broadening of the entire personality through the contact of his whole being with another culture, in this case with France.

There are many modern writers, from Mori Ōgai and Natsume Sōseki down to Mishima and Endo Shūsaku, whose spiritual and literary development involved just such a process. The study of that process remains an important one for comparative studies and one that might well be undertaken both to enlighten us about the meaning of the work of such particular authors and, perhaps more importantly, to help us understand the nature of real genius, which, as Stanislavsky suggested to his audience in Paris in 1922, extends beyond any frontier.

It seems appropriate, by way of example, to show something of the fresh flavor of Kishida's work that his early audiences found so appealing. The humor, fantasy, and sense of human dignity shown in Kishida's dramas were regarded by many of his early critics as deriving from a European inspiration, yet these qualities represented as much as anything else a homage by Kishida to the values in modern life he had located within himself through his contemplation of Europe. The freshness of language and interplay of personality shown in a play like the sketch that follows, *Buranko* (The Swing),[6] written in 1925, were new to the stage, yet already typical of the life of the period. Kishida's ability to capture the atmosphere of his time, at least insofar as it was reflected in the lives of the sophisticated urban dwellers of the kind often chronicled in the novels of Tanizaki Jun'-ichirō, makes this moment in the life of a young married couple seem surprisingly universal. Indeed, a Western reader need only be informed that Japanese breakfast menus differ from our own and that shoes are not normally worn in the house. The rest can be discovered, with some delight, for oneself.

THE SWING

Characters:

> HUSBAND
> WIFE
> KAMAKIRI, *a friend of the* HUSBAND

The living room   *Morning*

WIFE.   [*Laying out the breakfast things on a small table.*]
            It's time to get up, you know. Come on now!
HUSBAND.   [*Off stage.*] I'm up. What on earth is the time?
WIFE.   Every morning it's the same thing—you know, don't
            you?
HUSBAND.   Is it already that late?

WIFE. Now just what time do you think it is?

HUSBAND. [*As though leaping out of bed.*] Kamakiri hasn't shown up yet, has he?

WIFE. [*With some impatience.*] Calm down now . . . and with that loud voice . . .

HUSBAND. [*Appearing.*] Last night, you know, I had a really extraordinary dream.

WIFE. [*Not taking him up on it.*] Be careful. The tube of toothpaste has split open.

HUSBAND. [*On his way to the kitchen.*] Any rats in here? Last night, I mean . . .

WIFE. [*Her attention continues to focus on the top of the breakfast tray.*] Where did you put those things yesterday morning? You didn't go for a bath last night . . .

HUSBAND. [*Using a toothbrush.*] Well, maybe this is a good day for a bath.

WIFE. Too bad. Those vegetables I cooked day before yesterday seem spoiled already.

HUSBAND. Perhaps . . . You know, I've been dreaming a lot these days, but I've never had one as surprising as this.
[*Pause.*]
It really was delightful, that dream.

WIFE. Was there a towel in there?

HUSBAND. There was.
Just because it was a dream, you needn't just make fun of them.
As soon as I tell you something like this, right away you tell me that I mustn't depend on them.
But just because I dream I have become a millionaire, I don't really think I *have,* for heaven's sake. I'm not so foolish that I'd take *that* seriously.
[*Pause.*]
A dream is, well, always just a dream.
No question about it.
But you know, a real dream is quite different from a daydream.
A dream is something that happened sometime during your real life. It just comes to you naturally, while you're sleeping.

WIFE.   Now don't fuss at me if the leeks boil too long!

HUSBAND.   Oh . . . are we having leek soup for breakfast . . . I see
               . . . [*The sound of a face being washed; eventually, the* HUS-
               BAND *appears, wiping off his face with a towel. His* WIFE
               brings the kettle from the kitchen.]

WIFE.   We need to buy another rice tub, you know.

HUSBAND.   [*Hanging the towel on a peg, he sits in front of an oblong charcoal
               brazier.*]
               I feel like having a smoke.

WIFE.   Of course. Just make sure how much time you have.

HUSBAND.   [*Lighting his cigarette.*] There's nothing to worry about yet.
               [*As if looking outside.*] What a nice day . . .
               [*Pause.*]
               Actually, my curiosity about dreams has to do with how
               interesting they are.

WIFE.   [*Dishes up the rice.*]

HUSBAND.   Dreams are what save me from boredom. They teach me
               the real meaning of humanity.

WIFE.   [*Serves the soup.*]

HUSBAND.   Between yesterday and today . . . today and tomorrow
               . . . I take journeys that cost no money. Happy journeys.
               As far as I'm concerned, a dream is one part of reality.
               They aren't empty—like hopes . . . or ideals . . .

WIFE.   [*Picking up her chopsticks.*] You seem to dream so often,
               don't you?

HUSBAND.   Are you jealous? Now my dream last night . . . [*Picking
               up his chopsticks.*]

WIFE.   Before you get started on that, don't forget to bring
               home that travel allowance you have coming to you just
               as soon as you can.

HUSBAND.   Oh yes, right you are. Nine yen, seventy sen. I mustn't
               think I can dream that away too . . . I'll bring the
               money back with me today.
               [*Silence.*]

WIFE.   No eggs this morning.

HUSBAND.   Really? Why not?

WIFE.   I forgot to go out and buy them.

HUSBAND.   Oh! Well, if that's the way you want to put it.
               "I forgot."
               What a nice way of putting things that is . . .

Ugliness . . . gloom . . . suffering, fear . . . that word can cover them all.

Please forget . . . forget . . . whatever it is, forget it.

WIFE. [*Taking this rather badly.*] Well, I *did* really just forget them.

HUSBAND. So much the better! [*Pause.*] And what's more, the rice you cooked this morning was magnificent.

WIFE. [*Forcing herself to make a cheerful face.*] Well, the charcoal . . .

HUSBAND. [*Looking into his wife's face.*] Oh yes . . . I understand, of course.

WIFE. Really . . . ? [*Her eyes glisten with tears.*]

HUSBAND. Nonsense. The trouble with you is, you don't have any dreams. And when you do manage to have one, it invariably turns out to be uninteresting.

WIFE. But how do I know what sort of dream is supposed to be exciting?

HUSBAND. I see. Once, when I told you about a dream I had, I was so caught up in it that you didn't understand what I was talking about. And if you didn't understand, then it wouldn't seem interesting to you. Now the dream I had last night—you certainly will understand that one! Let me explain it so you will.

After all, you are my wife. You certainly want to know at least what kind of dreams your husband is having.

WIFE. [*Taking her husband's bowl, she fills it with rice.*]
Here, I've filled this up for you.

HUSBAND. Yes indeed!

WIFE. It's a long time until noon, and your stomach will get empty.

HUSBAND. [*Taking the bowl.*]
In the dream, I still seemed to be very young . . .
I mean, something like sixteen or seventeen . . .
It was a time in my life when the world seemed very lonely.
[*Pause.*]
As I always told you
I had nobody I could call a friend;
If you asked me how I amused myself,
Alone,
I might chase dragonflies.

In winter,
Back on the mountain slopes where the sun reached,
Every day, every day,
I sketched, drew pictures
Of the distant forest.
Those were my pleasures.

WIFE.   It's perfectly disgusting to put so much soy sauce on your food.

HUSBAND.   When I was a child, I put soy sauce on everything I ate.

WIFE.   It's bad for you.

HUSBAND.   With you, everything ends up that way.
Now, my dream.
I was aimless,
Wandering into the midst of the forest.
It was just the kind of forest I had painted every day.
It was night.
And just then . . .

WIFE.   Here, try these instead. [*Giving him some salted pickles.*]

HUSBAND.   Yes, it was night.
I went deep into the forest and looked
And the forest—the forest I painted
Had suddenly, somehow, become enormous, vast.
Like in Russia. Or South America.
Somewhere like that:
One of those huge, unexplored places.

WIFE.   [*Begins to speak.*]

HUSBAND.   Now just quiet down and listen.
It was night, and just then . . .
I didn't feel apprehensive at all.
No, not at all.

But unreasonably sad.

I suddenly thought I might commit suicide.

WIFE.   That is really quite enough. I think you've been taking it easy this morning for just about as long as you can afford to.

HUSBAND.   Don't worry—I want you to hear me through to the end.

I thought of suicide.

Then,
I noticed the branch of a tree:
Throwing my sash over, like a hook
And tying the ends above my head,
I thought to hang myself.

WIFE. [*Averting her face.*] How could you?
HUSBAND. Shall I go on?

I was ready to go ahead . . .

Suddenly, someone seemed to be tapping my shoulder from behind.

WIFE. There was someone there?
HUSBAND. Not only "someone." A lovely girl. She must have been twelve or thirteen.

Laughing, she seemed to be looking at me . . .
[*A pause. The* WIFE *takes her* HUSBAND's *rice bowl from his tray and puts it back in his hands again.*]

HUSBAND. She was looking at me.

I thought somehow, somewhere, I had met her before—
At least it seemed that way to me, but somehow,
I could not summon up the recollection.

WIFE. Later, you understood?
HUSBAND. Wait, don't get ahead of me.
[*Hurriedly, he stuffs in his food.*]

Just then, in a very friendly way, she asked me,
"What are you doing?"
I told her
I was making a swing.
"Let's ride it together," she said, and so I told her
My sash was too short for both of us.

WIFE. [*Bursts out laughing.*] Well now really . . .
HUSBAND. [*Looking very serious.*]
That's what I told her.

[*Pause.*]
Then she said,
"Tie mine to yours,"
And she undid her sash of red muslin.

WIFE.   [*Laughing.*] How distasteful!

HUSBAND.   She untied it.
[*Pause.*]
I really had no choice in the matter.
So I made the swing
And we both sat down.
[*Pause.*]
The tree trunk swayed unsteadily.
Above my head, I suddenly seemed to hear the shrill
    beating of wings:
All the birds of the forest seemed to cry out together.
The two of us,
Unawares,
Sitting in the swing,
Wrapped our arms around each other.

WIFE.   [*Gradually assuming a grimmer expression.*] Do you want your
tea now?

HUSBAND.   Ah, my tea.
[*Pause.*]
My tea, yes. But . . .

About what I was going to tell you, the fascinating thing
is that . . .

WIFE.   Go on with your story when you get home tonight. It's
time to put your shoes on and go.

HUSBAND.   Today I'll put on my "English bulldogs." They're
shined, aren't they?

WIFE.   [*Rising, gets out his suit.*]

HUSBAND.   [*Looking obliquely at his wife.*]

This time, I looked carefully, very carefully, at the girl's
face.
I did not know her. But she reminded me of someone.
Someone I saw somewhere, I must have met . . . or
talked to.

WIFE.   [*Looking over his socks for holes.*] You won't be taking your
            shoes off anywhere today, will you?
HUSBAND.   I don't think so . . . no, I'm sure not.
            In any case, I had seen her somewhere, someplace.
            Who do you think it was?
WIFE.   I understand perfectly well. And remember, your friend
            is waiting for you now.
HUSBAND.   No, come on, who do you think it was?
WIFE.   Whoever it was is a matter of complete indifference to
            me. You only talk over things in the morning, when there
            is so little time. This evening, you no doubt can explain
            all this to me in a more leisurely fashion.
HUSBAND.   Yes, in a more leisurely fashion.
            But then, my impressions will no longer be fresh.
            Now, in the morning, my dream is still clear,
            Bright, somewhere, in the back of my head . . .

            No, I don't think it can keep until then. Once I breathe
            in that dusty air in the office, the whole thing will be fin-
            ished.

            What a terrible place.

            But when I come back home and see you, I feel alive
            again.

            Alive, but . . . well, that's *all* I feel.

            The problem is, you see everything much too precisely.
            [*Pause.*]
            I'd better change now.

            Say, isn't Kamakiri late this morning?

            [*Draining his teacup, the* HUSBAND *gets up and begins taking off
            his kimono.*]
WIFE.   [*As she helps him.*] This will be too warm for you.
HUSBAND.   [*Singing in a curious little voice from the back of his throat.*]

Ta-ra-ra   ra-ra   ra-ra
Ta-ra-ra   ra-ra   ra-ra
Ta-ra-ra   ra-ra   ra-ra

WIFE.   [*Brushing the dust from his clothes and then, as if releasing him gently.*] What is it you're singing in that jumbled up fashion?

HUSBAND.   Jumbled up?

When it's a song you don't know, doesn't it always sound jumbled up?
[*Pause.*]
You said just now that you understood, didn't you?
The woman this girl looked like: who was she?
Isn't the whole thing a little odd?
How old were you when I first saw you?
Nineteen?
No, twenty?
Something like that, wasn't it?

When you were twelve or thirteen, what did you look like?
There's no way for me to know, you'll have to agree.

WIFE.   You could have seen some photographs.

HUSBAND.   Is that so?
Well, possibly.

I see you're still cool as a cucumber.
How delightful! Still . . .
If you haven't had any suspicions up until now . . .

Let me say first I want you to believe what a happy man I really am.

WIFE.   I . . . I am happy too.

HUSBAND.   Splendid. Splendid. That's the right attitude.
[*Pause.*]
Shall I go on?

That girl, somehow, resembled you.
No, more than that, she was your image.

In fact she was you altogether.
Now here is the really astonishing part of the dream:
When I realized this, I was neither surprised nor
    flustered.

I was sixteen.
You were twelve.
And I was holding you.
Calmly, quietly,
We passed the night on the swing . . .

WIFE.   Here's your vest.
HUSBAND.   The swing
Without any effort, moved easily . . .
[*Pause.*]
Each time you bent over me, your flowing hair tangled in
    my face.
You said it was delightful and brought your face closer to
    mine.

WIFE.   [*Laughing.*] Really? I did?
HUSBAND.   The swing
As though by itself,
Seemed to keep on swaying . . .
[*Pause.*]
The dawn light was shining through the leaves of the
    trees
Each time we looked up;
Now your face was bathed in silver.
I
Looked down, deeply, into your eyes.

And then . . . you were laughing . . .

WIFE.   [*Leaning her head on her husband's shoulder.*]
HUSBAND.   Then
You began to fall asleep.
And I began to drowse off as well.
[*A long silence.*]

And from then on, you know what happened as well as I!
Of course the world, the real world, seems quite different.

[*Pause.*]

So then . . . do you remember?

The next morning, we moved here, to this house.

And where are we now? [*He looks around the room.*]

Is this a real house for real human beings?

A house where real human beings love each other?

[*Pause.*]

It certainly wasn't last night.

What I thought was a forest is a palace.

What I thought was a swing is a soft, warm, suspension
    bed of velvet.

WIFE.   What is this suspension bed?

HUSBAND. Don't you know what a suspension bed is? Why, it's a
kind of cradle for adults.

WIFE.   And the palace?

HUSBAND. Well . . .

This palace is no ordinary fairy-tale sort of place.

[*The sound of knocking at the outer door.*]

VOICE.   Hey! Aren't you ready yet?

WIFE.   [*Flustered, leaving her husband's shoulder.*] Now look at that,
you're late again.

HUSBAND. [*Intimidated, buttoning his vest.*] No, no, I'm not late. [*In a
loud voice.*] What's all this? Are you going now? Some-
how, I thought you were taking the day off . . .

VOICE.   What's all that?

[*The owner of the voice sticks his head in the room.*]

WIFE.   Oh, you shouldn't come into this mess . . . !

KAMAKIRI. [*To the* HUSBAND.] I see you got back safe from your trip.

[*To the* WIFE.] Good morning, ma'am.

WIFE.   However I try to rush him, the results are always the
same.

HUSBAND. Everything is just fine.

Now listen to the rest of the story. This palace I was telling you about is no ordinary run-of-the-mill palace.

WIFE.   [*Helping him on with his coat.*] You've got the buttons
wrong. Higher.

HUSBAND. Maybe the word "palace" isn't really the right one after

all. I mean, the decorations are just for the people who
live there.

KAMAKIRI. This all sounds very interesting. But can you have decorations like that?

HUSBAND. Of course. In the first place, the suspension bed is quite
out of the ordinary. And of course the swing too.
Why . . .

KAMAKIRI. What swing are you talking about?

HUSBAND. What swing?

WIFE. It is very naughty of you, Mr. Kamakiri, to listen in to all
this. And with such a straight face. [*To her* HUSBAND.]
Come on. That's enough now.

KAMAKIRI. What on earth are you all talking about?

WIFE. It's only a dream . . . *his* dream. As usual . . .
[*She gives her* HUSBAND *his handkerchief, watch, and wallet.*]

KAMAKIRI. What? Is that what's going on?

HUSBAND. Now look here, you're the kind of man who can understand when a dream is interesting. But I can't imagine
you having any of them yourself.

KAMAKIRI. Never have them. Which reminds me, I'd like to ask
your wife . . .

HUSBAND. Let me ask you. Have you ever ridden on a swing?

KAMAKIRI. No, I haven't. In fact . . .

HUSBAND. Fine, fine, I'll hear about all that later. Now I'm talking
to you about a dream I had last night.

[*Lighting a cigarette.*]

You see, when I was about seventeen . . . at that age,
the world seemed, in some strange way, to be a very sad
place . . .
[*Moving toward the door.*]
It was a time when one comes to learn so many things,
even without realizing it . . .
[*He vanishes offstage.*]

KAMAKIRI. [*To the* HUSBAND.] You know, I'm a bit concerned about
you.

HUSBAND'S VOICE. Why? There's no reason to be . . .

WIFE. [*Goes to see her* HUSBAND *off.*]

KAMAKIRI. [*Without making a gesture to get up; his words seem directed to the* HUSBAND, *but the feelings behind them are to the* WIFE.] Listen, I just got word that my father is suddenly coming down from the country. I don't mind that at all, but . . .

HUSBAND'S VOICE. Let's go, let's go . . .

KAMAKIRI. I'm coming. Ma'am, what would you think if tonight . . .

HUSBAND'S VOICE. Yes, yes, everything will work out. But first [*as if pulling his friend's hand*] come on and listen to my dream.

KAMAKIRI. [*Gets up, then disappears from view.*] But ma'am . . .

HUSBAND'S VOICE. Come on. She's not involved at all.

WIFE'S VOICE. Well . . . [*Suddenly surprised.*] Well, have a good day then!

[*The sound of a door being closed.*]

WIFE. [*Returning to the stage, she sits down facing the brazier and puts her chin on her hands. Spontaneously, a delicate smile comes over her face.*]

HUSBAND'S VOICE. You see, I was sixteen at the time . . .
And the world,
In some strange way . . .
Say, where are we going?

KAMAKIRI'S VOICE. Wait a minute. This is urgent . . .

HUSBAND'S VOICE. Oh for heaven's sake . . . well hurry up about it. There are people coming . . .

[*There begins, from no particular place, the sound of the two men whistling, quite out of tune with each other; for an instant, the two sounds can be heard mingling together.*]

Curtain

II

THE THEATRE
AS PILGRIMAGE

4

Mokuami's Evil One and Her Modern Counterpart

THE EUROPEAN art scholar E. H. Gombrich, whose work I have read with profit for many years, often stresses as a fundamental principle his conviction that art is basically constructed from art, and that the most useful avenue to understand the meaning and significance of any particular work may well be to look at the art from which it has been derived. That principle seems to me to be profoundly true. In more than one sense, the two plays about which I want to comment here can serve to illustrate Gombrich's point most eloquently.

In the theatre the specifics of contemporary life, represented both by the actors who perform and, in some cases, the subject matter chosen by the playwright, enter into the realm of art even more quickly and more directly than in the visual arts. In particular the fact that *kabuki* playwrights often wrote their plays as though they were functioning as journalists, recording and commenting on the immediate social scene, offered them a peculiar challenge. Turning the equivalent of headlines into art, art that was acceptable to their public, involved a special creative process that, if properly studied, can tell us as much about the society as can the plays themselves. In the theatre, the audience must immediately accept the experience they witness; the artistic version of reality they are shown must somehow appear as naturally self-validating to them. It is this process by which the playwright selects and shapes his material, with his various responsibilities to artistic tradition, contemporary truth, and his own intuition, that defines his accomplishment in the context of these circumstances. In terms of *kabuki,* this process has not, insofar as I know, been carefully charted. Until it has been, we, as contemporary spectators, readers, or students of Japanese culture, may risk making judgements on the theatrical effectiveness or on the literary value of a text on the basis of the wrong premises. Concerning this issue, too complex to be dealt with in all its aspects here, I only wish to provide an example, a question, and a comment.

My example consists of two plays that take as their subject matter the career of a famous murderess and criminal of the early Meiji period, a woman named Takahashi Oden (1841–1880). She was born in the Jōshū area north of Tokyo (now Gumma Prefecture), and, as the standard Japanese biographical account would have it, was brought up in such an atmosphere of poverty and degradation that the development of her "unlucky character" was doubtless inevitable. Her foster father arranged for her marriage to a fellow villager, a man who had contracted leprosy; she disposed of him and then went on to enjoy a series of paramours until she was apprehended for stealing. When her other crimes were proven, she was tried and sentenced to death. One of the most celebrated criminals of her day, she was usually referred to as a "Jezibel" *(yofu)* or "vampire" *(dokufu),* and her grisly career became the subject of a number of stories, including a prose account by the early Meiji essayist Kanagaki Robun and, more importantly for the present purposes, of a play by the last of the great *kabuki* playwrights, Kawatake Mokuami (1816–1893). Mokuami based his drama on various contemporary accounts and on a report of matters brought up at the trial itself. His play, *Tōjiawase Oden no kanabumi* (A Notebook Sewn Together on Oden) was written in 1880, the same year in which she died. It was an enormous success.

In 1979, almost a hundred years later, the contemporary playwright Yashiro Seiichi (born 1927), one of the leading postwar writers for the Japanese theatre, read an account of Oden and decided to create his own theatrical version of her lurid career.[1] Yashiro, who has developed and sustained a remarkable talent for depicting the language, speech, and psychology of Edo in a number of accomplished plays written during the past twenty years, doubtless found the subject altogether appropriate for his own special artistic and moral stance. "My play is my own requiem for a woman who set out to deny her fate."[2] Yashiro's play is entitled *Dokufu no chichi—Takahashi Oden,* "The Father of the Vampire—Takahashi Oden." The change in emphasis revealed in his title indicates Yashiro's interest in the complex relationship between Oden and her foster father, onto whom the author shifts much of the responsibility for her conduct.

Both Mokuami and Yashiro follow the same story line, yet the impressions given by the two plays are entirely different. I have seen the original production of the Yashiro play in Tokyo but have not as yet seen the *kabuki* version staged; still, even a reading of the Mokuami text indicates at once, artistically speaking, an enormous gap between the two. Some variation is certainly to be expected, as each playwright was working in a different theatrical tradition. In 1880, Mokuami was writing for a still-stylized theatre, using male actors for all the parts, making full use of a long musical and dramatic tradition of which, indeed, he was the last great exemplar. Yashiro, a hundred years later, was writing in a modern theatrical tradition enriched by heavy and presumably healthy doses of Ibsen, Strindberg, Chekhov, and Pirandello; Yashiro, too, has himself made a self-conscious reevaluation of the artistry of the traditional Japanese theatre in many of his own works. Nevertheless, an examination of the disparity between the two versions of the same theatrical biography reveals a great deal about the differences between the society of early Meiji and that of the present day. This sort of artistic sociology can, in turn, help explain the diversities in treatment of Oden in both plays and so suggest the artistic limits within which both playwrights chose to work. These unarticulated assumptions on the part of the two writers have at least as much to do with the shaping of their work as do their own conscious artistic purposes.

Both playwrights, in shaping their material, have one crucial demand made upon them: they must make credible the murders, and thus the murderer, to their respective audiences. A raw account of the career of Oden is merely shocking. Without some artistic transformation, such a bald narrative cannot in and of itself provide the basis for a satisfying dramatic experience.

Yashiro, who studied the Mokuami version, refers to the earlier play in the prologue to his own and suggests that it represented a response by the earlier playwright to a "taste for the bizarre" in his audiences. Mokuami's play is in seven sprawling acts, some with multiple scenes, ranging in location from a hot spring resort and a farmer's hut in Jōshū to the final scenes in Yokohama, a Tokyo court, and a prison cell. Most of the locales are shady and have a sort of dour gangster glamor that, in some odd way, must have had the same fascination to *kabuki* audiences that Brecht's slums have provided in *The Threepenny Opera* for modern middle-class audiences. Mokuami's play sustains a powerful atmosphere, and the dialogue on the whole is both salty and realistic, far different from the sort of speech familiar to Western students of *bunraku* puppet theatre texts and *kabuki* in, say, the more classic seventeenth-century plays of Chikamatsu. Indeed, in many ways Mokuami, from the vantage point of a contemporary reader at least, seems more skillful at rendering actual speech than some of the "realistic" new-style *shingeki* playwrights who twenty years after the *kabuki* playwright's death were already beginning an attempt to re-create Ibsen in Japanese terms.

Mokuami's play was, of course, contemporary with the events portrayed. Yashiro, a hundred years later, was writing a history play. To use the traditional terminology, the category thus changes from a *sewamono*, a contemporary domestic play, to a *jidaimono*, or history play, which suggests many shifts in psychology and style. Yashiro is always conscious of the historicity of his material, and his use of a slightly quaint atmosphere that he and doubtless his spectators find in the manners of Meiji Japan is well evidenced by his narrator's mention of the Mokuami play, the choice of settings and costumes, and so forth. This aspect of Yashiro's fascination with historical color doubtless culminates in the scene in which Oden is visited by her prostitute mother, dressed in splendid Western Victorian dress.

Yashiro's play is much shorter than Mokuami's and is constructed in a series of scenes in which the points of view of a number of the more important characters are presented, in order to shed light on the character of Oden herself. Yashiro, as does Mokuami, makes good use of the various lurid events in Oden's career; his text moves in and out of monologue to create a trim and often gripping series of stage pictures that never fail to hold the spectator's psychological as well as visual attention. Like Mokuami, Yashiro finishes with courtroom and prison scenes.

Yashiro's strategy to validate the character of Oden is very different from that chosen by Mokuami. Toward the end of the play, Yashiro creates a scene in which Oden is given a long, rambling, and revealing soliloquy, in which she in effect explains herself to the audience, now prepared to form some judgements about the honesty of those self-revelations. Oden sits alone in the rain and ponders to herself over her own past. What follows are a few random excerpts from that long scene.

ODEN. That man. What did he explain to me that night? About my own body . . . ? Yes, he said that I was—what was the word?—*carnal*. And not just that I work for it. That I was born that way. My natural temperament. I suppose that I must have my mother to thank for it. She's the one who bore me. Yes, thank her. I thought that I should see my mother once. I have always wanted to meet her. Anyway, I suppose she's dead on the road someplace. It would be just like my mother. Actually, I really am grateful to her . . . Still, a woman who is *carnal:* it suddenly occurs to me how hard it is to be like that and still go on leading your life, day by day. Yes, it's true. Your body can't stand being alive without a man. As for the men, they call it prostitution; but although they despise me, when they do manage to make love to me, I seem to make their lives worth living for them. Even the sort of man who would think he couldn't be saved no matter if he prayed to the gods and buddhas all day long, without a stop—even a man like that will say that he is saved by me. There have been so many like that. My foster father. And my patron, Ushimatsu.

Well then. Am I the kind of woman who was brought into the world for the sake of men? . . . but if I thought I were some sort of lifelong mother goddess of mercy . . . troublesome, it's all become very troublesome. As far as I'm concerned, any man has been all right, as long as he's a man. Any bag of horse's bones. As long as I was physically satisfied, it was all right. I suppose I was using men as a kind of tool.[3]

Later, she concludes:

If I had to answer frankly, really frankly, I would have to say that what my spirit wants my body does not want. And no one will listen. And what my spirit rejects, my body demands. It wants to try anything. And why should this be so? Why? Yes, why?[4]

Yashiro provides a remarkable glimpse into the character of his heroine, and provides his audience as well with a scene that is satisfying, validating if you will, because it seems so in line with our contemporary attitudes and judgements concerning the way in which women traditionally have been used, and misused, by men. Needless to say, Oden's own view of herself, and her questions about herself, are considerably different from the attitudes held about her by those around her; Yashiro, in the total construction of the play, has given a Pirandello-like, or perhaps I should say a *Rashōmon*-like, view of the truth. Still, Oden's own view remains at the center of the play and she is, as this scene shows, in touch with her own real feelings as Yashiro has decided to re-create them.

From the vantage point of this kind of contemporary treatment, a look back at the Mokuami play produces a sense of profound surprise. No scene in which the inner character of Oden is examined, explained, or revealed, is included. Indeed, from the general construction of the play, which reveals clearly the enormous skill shown by Mokuami in every aspect of his composition, it is quite clear that none was thought to be necessary. Concerning Oden's interior life there is only silence. We are shown various lurid events, but never her thoughts or comments upon them. This is not to suggest in any way that Mokuami's Oden is not a theatrically effective character. The role is a highly evocative one. The scene at her trial is particularly brilliant and would give a first-class performer a peerless opportunity on the stage. For much of the lengthy scene, Oden attempts to bluff the judges and refuses to admit that she has committed any crime at all. Perhaps a few lines can suggest something of the quality of the whole.

> *Oden enters, carried on stage in a bamboo palanquin. The jailers carry her to the center of the stage. She makes a point of appearing ill. She stares at the judge.*

JUDGE. Oden. You have been sick since last year. But the fact that you evidently cannot walk today gives the impression that the situation is grave indeed.

ODEN. When I learned that I was suspected of murder, I was sorely afflicted. I became ill. Then, as I was unable to walk, I had this seat turned into a sort of litter. I do hope that you will forgive this impertinence.[5]

As the witnesses begin to testify, she cries in pain every time an accusation is made.

JUDGE.   On the basis of all this proof, can everything that has been said about what has happened since last year still be considered a lie?

ODEN.   That. That, well . . .

JUDGE.   Proofs concerning each of these matters can be put before you, one by one.

ODEN.   That. That . . . well . . .

JUDGE.   Any falsehood will reveal a discrepancy.

ODEN.   Ha.

JUDGE.   What do you have to say?

ODEN.   Ha.

JUDGE.   If you have anything to say, say it.

ODEN.   Ha.

JUDGE.   Well?

ODEN.   Ah, how in pain I am.[6]

In this scene, Oden puts on quite a show for the court. The combination of servility and defiance Mokuami has created in her provides brilliant material for the stage performance of a criminal. Yet in the following scene, in which the dramatist depicts Oden's final days in prison, the tonality of the play changes altogether. Much of Oden's language becomes poetic. She asks forgiveness for what she has done and says that she can now go to her death "with no regrets." Here are a few passages from that long scene.

ODEN.   [*To her father.*] . . . gradually, in time, the authorities began to recognize that proofs of my evil schemes were piling up; today at the trial, when I was told that I was to be hanged, I received the retribution for all the lies I have told and the trouble I have caused them for three years. Such is the punishment that Oden has received from heaven. Indeed, things could have happened in no other way. I realize that I tried to cheat and to escape from the authorities, who ask into human right and wrong. I tried to bring about, using a weak woman's logic, what could not be accomplished. And that is not all: I have shown a lack of filial piety toward my parent, who cannot now face the world because of my conduct. How detestable all of this is. Please think that, somehow, all of this must have been caused by the karma of a previous life, and, somehow, forgive me.[7]

A character has turned into a cipher and risks cliché. Her last lines confirm the process.

ODEN.   My wickedness is deep: passing across the River of Three Crossings, my body will doubtless wither away at the Mountain of Swords
FATHER. Then good-bye, for:
ODEN.   This is our final parting in this world.[8]

In these final moments, the assumptions of proper artistic closure seemingly employed by Mokuami permit the specificity of his character to dissolve into generalities of language and sentiment. To our contemporary sensibility, Yashiro's play is wholly credible. Mokuami's remains remote.

Such, then, are the data I would use to pose questions concerning the reciprocal nature of the relationship between the theatre and the society that produces it. Any such relationship is difficult to examine in depth without more extensive evidence than can be marshalled in this brief essay. I would, however, like to offer some suggestions as to where one might begin. One point, of course, is clear: Mokuami's abilities as a dramatist are not at issue. Therefore in order to understand, and perhaps ultimately make a judgement on, his artistic accomplishments, we must come to know his purposes. And in order to investigate those purposes, I believe, one of the most useful places to begin is to examine the nature of his audiences.

Since the 1920s a number of European literary historians and critics have studied the changing relationships between audience, writer, and theatre in European culture, and some of their generalizations can be useful in attempting to relate the various complex factors required to understand the often unarticulated importance of these connections. Although the specifics in the Japanese case are, as in all cases, unique, the generalizations offered on the basis of European theatre are often provocative and helpful. In this instance, I have two particular theoreticians in mind. The first of them, Georg Lukàcs, has this to say about the theatre in his book *The Historical Novel*.

The dramatic factors in life as such, however, as independent, heightened segments of the life process, are necessarily public in *every* society. . . . Almost every fact of life may, under certain conditions, manifest itself at sufficiently high a level to acquire a public character; it has a side which concerns the public *directly,* which requires a public for its representation. Precisely here we see the transformation of quantity and quality very clearly. Dramatic conflict is not distinguished from other events in life by its social content, but by the manner in which contradictions sharpen and the degree to which they do so. This sharpening then produces a new, original quality.[9]

In other words, in order to be effective, the tension between ordinary life as perceived by the audience and the peculiarities of the dramatic event presented by the playwright must be real, and the connection between the two must be sustained. By this definition, then, the career of Takahashi Oden provides a suitable example of the material for an effective play: the events are true and, no matter how peculiar, are not altogether removed from the possibilities of life that could be imagined by Mokuami's audiences.

To this concept Lukàcs adds another, that of the gradual movement of audience concern from the communal to the private. Lukàcs uses a Marxist vocabulary, but his point can be acknowledged without reference to that particular rhetoric.

With the growing social division of labor and the complication of social relations in class societies, a division between the public and the private occurs in life itself. Literature as a reflection of life cannot help reproducing this process. . . . Dramatic form stands or falls with the direct public character specific to it. Thus [at a time when this division has become more and more crucial], drama must either disappear from life, or, in unfavorable circumstances, attempt to give portrayal in its own way to the public elements still present in social life, but it will have to struggle with unfavorable material as it were, against the current.[10]

For Lukàcs, the assumptions formerly held by audiences are now fragmented, and their responses can be explained, and justified, in a way that was not formerly a part of any communal aesthetic. Rather, according to Lukàcs, the modern playwright is required to examine the psychology and actions of his characters in a new way in an attempt to match these new expectations.

In line with this argument, the French sociologist Jean Duvignaud has insisted that the audience in the theatre wishes to project its own credibility onto the play that it witnesses. "This capacity of a group to create life from an obscure spectacle in different social frameworks reaches its peak in what we call the theatre: the aesthetic experience seems to satisfy a fundamental need for groups to project their credibility, their 'expectancy' into the forms it reproduces."[11] By this analysis it is the audience that imposes meaning on the events it witnesses on the stage, and the spectators "test their own existence" in terms of their reactions to what they observe. Thus, for Duvignaud, in a society that still retains a sense of communal values, the basic assumptions of society, and so those of the audience, are simply taken for granted. The artistic response is that which validates such unspoken assumptions. If, in the case of Tokugawa Japan, social order is the assumption, and *kanzenchōaku* (praise the good, punish the bad) the artistic mechanism, then Duvignaud's model would seem highly suggestive. Oden's final lines can be seen to serve as a reaffirmation, and the poetry of her final scene as an artistic means, by which the audience can come to terms with events that ordinary social morality quite simply deems inadmissible. Such an analysis is not extreme. One only needs to think of a most obvious Western analogue—the end of *Hamlet,* for example—when bizarre behavior and multiple murder are explained, and explained away, in terms of a rent in the social order that can now be healed again.

HORATIO.   And let me speak to th'yet unknowing world
                    How these things came about: so shall you hear
                    Of carnal, bloody, and unnatural acts,
                    Of accidental judgements, casual slaughters;
                    Of deaths put on by cunning and forc'd cause,
                    And, in this upshot, purposes mistook
                    Fall'n on th'inventors' heads; all this can I
                    Truly deliver.[12]

Shakespeare's language of healing is different, certainly, from that of Mokuami, and it is spoken by a subsidiary character, not by the protagonist; nevertheless, Oden's acknowledgement of her own wickedness shows every bit as much the playwright's unforced homage to the appropriate social rhetoric. The fixed sentiments in both plays serve similar ends.

In the case of Yashiro's play, on the other hand, the audience is presumably composed of spectators with the kind of internalized, individualized sensibilities that Lukàcs sees as normative because of the development of the kind of political and social system that has become as much a part of contemporary Japan as it has of Europe or the United States. A retreat into an older artistic tradition, into the ancient poetic rhetoric of Buddhist salvation and damnation, is no longer effective. Yashiro, in order to compose a drama that will validate Oden to his contemporary audience, turns instead to psychology and the juxtaposition of differing social attitudes. His theme is thus to be the very ambiguity that Mokuami was at pains to shun. From the perspective of such students of literature as Lukàcs and Guignard, the change is inevitable, given the shifting nature of the audience and the society which they in turn represent.

Juxtaposing these two dramas, dealing as they do with a similar theme, is one way—although surely not the only way—to find the materials that can help us come to terms with making a judgement, finally, about the literary success of both writers and to help avoid any false disappointments concerning the accomplishments of Mokuami. Of course, examined from a contemporary point of view, a play like Mokuami's may seem to lack in certain crucial scenes precisely the kind of sharp characterization that we in this century enjoy, indeed demand. A look at both texts side by side is thereby helpful in that the aesthetic of Yashiro, potentially quite familiar to us, helps us to understand that of Mokuami, which decidedly is not.

At the beginning of this essay, I mentioned that I also wanted to make a comment on both plays, which brings me back to Mr. Gombrich's dictum that art basically grows out of art. Yashiro studied the Mokuami play closely and even quotes it in his text; in a real sense, Yashiro's version is a "translation" of the early play into modern language and psychology. In that regard, the artistic continuum is obvious. From the vantage point of comparative theatre, however, the lines seem clearer still. Neither play is realistic. Mokuami's atmosphere and dialogue are symbolic and poetic, and in the high movements of the play, the characters take on a friezelike quality, Puvis de Chavannes *à la Japonaise.* Yashiro, on the other hand, in composing what was for him a history play, creates a self-conscious atmosphere in which that historic moment, and the consciousness by his audience of that moment, plays an important part in creating in the spectators an emotional acceptance of what passes on the stage, *grand guignol* and psychological soliloquy alike. Indeed, a self-consciousness of the artifice of the theatre which has provided such an important element of the great Japanese theatrical tradition is common to both. Yashiro's play could not have been written if Japanese society had not changed and if Japanese playwrights of the preceding generations had not prepared their audiences through their ingestion of the methods of Ibsen, Chekhov, and certainly in this case Pirandello. Yet, even given the difference in method, Yashiro's commitment to theatricality, as opposed to realism, is as great as Mokuami's. His interest in what, writing about *kabuki,* Earl Ernst has called "presentational theatre," as opposed to Western "representational theatre," is every bit as basic as that of his predecessor. In this sense, the making of art from art, no matter what the shifts in society and sensibility may be, accounts for the strengths of both plays, and of the tradition that lies behind them.

5

Japanese Theatre
Language as Pilgrimage

WHEN I first began to attend performances by Japanese contemporary theatre companies in the 1950s, I was puzzled by what I took to be a disparity between the power of the texts chosen for performance and the quality of the acting available to make those texts come alive on the stage. To see Pirandello, Molière, and Kinoshita on the stage in Japan was a rare opportunity, and yet the performances, for all their polish, seemed to lack any real natural elegance. The thoughts that follow here, in fact, have grown from that initial sense of surprise and, perhaps, of disappointment.

The first help I received came in the form of a few paragraphs in Peter Arnott's *The Theatres of Japan*. Arnott, an expert on the Greek classic theatre who visited Japan in 1966, revealed his conception of an important distinction he found between Japanese and Western performing technique.

The gulf between the Japanese theatre and its Western counterpart embraces more than different social standards and unfamiliar subject-matter. They are two forms built on different aesthetic foundations, and divided by the actor's concept of his relation to his role. The extrovert and presentational style cultivated for centuries in Japan cannot be easily reconciled with plays written for actors trained in a different mode and expected to identify themselves psychologically with their roles. This is the most serious difficulty that the Japanese actor has to face. He is forced, in effect, to relearn the fundamentals of his trade. Japanese actors, on the whole, are more secure in Western plays to which the traditional methods can be applied. They are conspicuously successful in the "epic" style cultivated by Brecht and others, which comes close to, and indeed borrowed from, their own traditions. The

71

"alienation effect" demanded by Brecht from his characters is founded
on the premises of presentational acting. But the wholly naturalistic
style continues to elude them, with results sometimes disastrous to the
play. In Brecht, the [Japanese] actor is moving in a world he knows.[1]

Arnott's suggestion of a profound difference in craft and style
seemed to go a long way in answering my question; as it turned out,
however, his explanations opened up further questions still. When I
translated for an American production a drama by the contemporary
playwright Yamazaki Masakazu, one of the most thoughtful and
intellectually imaginative writers of his generation, the director, musing over the English script, told me that he was struck by the form in
which the drama was cast. "Why," he asked me, "should a contemporary playwright choose to write a metaphysical melodrama? The
play is extremely effective, but it is cast in a form difficult for American actors and based on assumptions difficult for us to seek out."

The director's remarks seemed most perceptive; and even though I
could not answer his question properly, I realized that perhaps he
was struck not so much by a need to search out different acting styles
but by the fact that an altogether different view of reality was suggested by this and the other Japanese plays he had read, a genuine
reality certainly, but one not based on the concept of mimesis so
familiar in Western drama since its very beginnings. Reality in the
Japanese theatre was to be found not in imitation but in stylization,
the kind of intense simplification and suggestiveness that had so
attracted certain important Western poets, composers, and writers to
the Japanese traditional theatre. How, then, was the stylization that
had so appealed to artists such as Claudel, Britten, Brecht, and Yeats
to be understood?

Various angles of analysis seemed possible. One obvious point,
and one well understood by Yeats, for example, was that this stylization seemed allied to ritual and could thus provide a means to allow
an audience an experience quite outside their everyday comprehension of themselves. The medieval *nō* drama shows this ability consis-
tently. An examination of ritual, in turn, can help show the purposes
of stylization. In seeking out the psychological basis of ritual, I was
led to the work of Victor Turner, mentioned earlier in this book; his
discussion of pilgrims leaving their orthodox social environments in
order to undergo a special experience, their assumption of voluntary

status as pilgrims, and their movements through symbolic time, all in order to seek the state of *communitas,* a universal sense of nonduality, which releases the pilgrim from his everyday "role playing and all its guilts," struck me as highly suggestive of the process through which an audience, albeit an ideal audience, might go.

But to what extent can the theatre be considered a place of pilgrimage? After all, the audience does not participate but rather watches and observes. Still, I thought, a case might be made out that the audience is always on a pilgrimage of sorts. I was reminded of a scene in Paul Claudel's play *L'Échange,* in which some of the qualities Turner points out as typical of a pilgrimage—a strange sense of time, of place, and the possibility of transcendental understanding—are placed in the province of the theatre. Lechy Elbernon is an actress, and at one point in the drama she is attempting to explain the craft of the theatre to a friend.

LECHY.   The theatre. Don't you know what it is?

MARTHE.   No.

LECHY.   There is a stage, there is an audience. In the evening, everything's closed. They all come, and they sit in rows, one behind the other, and they look.

MARTHE.   What do they look at, if everything is shut?

LECHY.   They look at the curtain. And what is behind it when it rises.

            And something happens on the stage just as though it were real.

MARTHE.   But it isn't real! It's like a dream you have when you're asleep.

LECHY.   Yes, that is why they come to the theatre at night . . .

            I look at them, the audience; and they are living, clothed flesh.

            And they cluster on the walls like flies, right up to the ceiling;

            I see those hundreds of white faces.

            Man lives his life in boredom, and ignorance that has clung to him from his birth,

            And because he does not know how anything begins or ends he goes to the theatre.

            And he looks at himself, his hands on his knees.

> And he laughs and he cries and cannot bear to leave . . .
> They look and listen as though they were asleep.
>
> MARTHE. The eye is made to see, and the ear to hear the truth.
> LECHY. What is truth? Is it not like an onion, wrapped in
>   seventeen skins?
> Who can see things as they are? The eye sees, the ear
>   hears,
> But only the mind can know. And that is why man
> Longs to take out what he carries in his mind and spirit
> To see it with his eyes and know it with his ears.
> And so it is that I show myself on the stage.[2]

Audiences, Claudel suggests, exist in a special state of heightened, detached awareness that is altogether reminiscent of Turner's psychological pilgrim state: dream as reality, time at a stop, the world of the spirit dominating the rule of the senses. In Claudel's vision, an audience comes to the theatre in the hope that its members can make manifest, to actually see before them, what may otherwise exist only inside their own souls, as potential. The spectators, desiring an understanding of themselves, seek that vision in the images they find in their own minds and souls, which are thrown up on the stage for them to examine, to look at and observe. In Turner's terms the spectators participate vicariously in the movement of the images on the stage that parade before them; they *see* the pilgrimage spread out before them.

If such a vicarious pilgrimage can be posited in terms of the theatre, then an examination of the nature of the relationship of an audience to the drama of its time can suggest as well what images a given audience may most desire to see, what kind of mirror it most wishes to have thrown up before it: in short, what kind of reflected pilgrimage it may find itself most wanting to seek out. Individuals, audiences, and societies change, and so will the nature of the pilgrimages on which they embark. By way of example I would like to indicate Japanese dramas from three historical periods that can suggest the dynamics of this process. All reveal a congruence with Turner's scheme: the pilgrimages seem to involve a voluntary act on the part of the pilgrim, the trip to a special place, and a segment of symbolic time. Finally, Turner's idea of a crucial liminal experience, a sense of *communitas,* seems present as well. To anticipate my conclusions, I would like in particular to suggest that a play written as a surrogate pilgrimage surely requires a style of composition and performance at variance with the kind of realism so basic to the modern Western theatre.

My first example is taken from the medieval *nō;* closest to European medieval ritual as these dramas are, they provide almost a paradigm for a dramatic version of Turner's conception of pilgrimage. The play I have chosen is one I have translated and the text of which I have studied closely, *Taema,*[3] a play attributed to the greatest figure in the history of *nō,* Zeami Motokiyo (1363–1443). The audiences for *nō* in Zeami's time were largely popular, with a sprinkling of aristocrats, not unlike the medieval popular audiences in Europe. Whatever the differences in class outlook, the audiences were held together by their common cultural consciousness, which centered on Buddhist belief and psychology. The texts of this and most other plays contain "high" sections of metaphysical poetry, presumably for the highly literate aristocrats, and "low" sections of easier prose for the commoners.

The play is a perfect model of a spiritual journey. The *waki,* or subsidiary character, consists of a priest, plus his two companions; the *shite,* or main character, appears first as a nun, then in the second part of the play as the Princess Chūjō. At the beginning of the play, the priests visit Taema temple to see the famous woven mandala there (which, incidentally, modern tourists can do as well, since the original temple, with its beautiful grounds, is about one hour from Osaka by train). They meet an old woman, a Buddhist nun, who is accompanied by a young girl. The pair tell the priest and his companions how Princess Chūjō prayed at the temple for the coming of Amida Buddha, and how eventually an aged nun had come to the princess, revealed herself as a manifestation of Amida, and heralded the princess' ascent to paradise. The nun and the girl next reveal themselves to the priest as dream-visions of the princess and Amida, then disappear. During the interlude, a farmer in the vicinity retells the story in simple language, adding the fact that Amida Buddha had presented a mandala woven of lotus threads to the princess. In the final and highly poetic section of the play, the priest and his companions pray for enlightenment; the princess now reappears in dazzling attire and reveals a poetic image of paradise. She praises Amida, presents the priest with a sutra, and bids him pray. As he kneels to do so, the vision fades.

The play follows Turner's schemata closely. The very opening lines of the play show the priests anxious to make a trip toward enlightenment.

PRIESTS. [*Together.*] Wonderful the Gate
                       Of the Wonderful Law:
                       Let us follow the road it discloses.[4]

The priest and his companions have consciously sought out a holy place, a sacred spot, far out of the way; their piety in turn makes it possible for them to identify the two others, the nun and the young girl, who also worship Amida Buddha. Their encounter together suggests the possibility of a shared *communitas,* a oneness that surpasses the individual.

GIRL.   Amida with a single mind
          Shows the way . . .
BOTH.   Let us never neglect
          To say with all our hearts,
          "I put my faith in Amida."
NUN.   And as we praise him,
          All distinction between the Buddha and ourselves
          Will disappear . . .[5]

They identify their own pilgrimage as a transcendental one.

NUN.   In that road which leads towards
          Cool purity
          We place our trust.[6]

As the priest and his companions observe these two women, the visitors come to realize that they are beginning to become involved in an experience that may lead them to still greater faith. The nun and the girl describe the various holy relics to be seen at Taema temple, then remind the priests of the proper attitude needed to participate in a real pilgrimage.

TOGETHER. Many are the well-known places,
Many the occasions to contemplate the Buddha
And to hear the Wonderful Law,
But too profound for our comprehension.
As a single strand of pure lotus,
Our cry rises from our united hearts,
Amida save us![7]

Mere observation, cognition, must be abandoned for the deep cry of faith. The nun now explains to the rapt priest how Princess Chūjō herself made a pilgrimage to the deep mountains, giving herself up to contemplation and prayers to Amida. As they finish the story, the two reveal themselves.

TOGETHER. We are transformed beings from the past,
A nun and a girl,
Who appeared in your dream,
And even as we speak these words
CHORUS. Light thrusts,
Flowers fall,
Miraculous odors everywhere,
Voices of music.[8]

Now the priest and his companions fulfill the third of Turner's conditions leading to *communitas:* they will come to move in symbolic time. In the final section of the play, as they begin their prayers to Amida, they are rewarded by a vision that might be classed as a form of extended reality, which will move them toward a transcendent experience.

PRIESTS. Even before we can speak of it,
How surprising!
Wondrous music sounds,
Light floods down,
Boddhisattvas,
Singing, dancing,
Before our eyes,
Sacred manifestations—
Wonderful, oh wonderful.[9]

The princess now appears and tells the priests of the joys of paradise.

CHORUS.   Wondrous Paradise!
              Magnificence, a vast unending world of sky
              Dazzles the sight, lost in paths of clouds.
PRINCESS.   The sound of the voice
              Of the turning wheel of the Wonderful Law
              Fills the air to the vast edges of Paradise.
CHORUS.   The heart, calm and quiet as the dawn
PRINCESS.   Is guided on its cool path to Paradise
              By the light of Amida.[10]

She then presents the priest with a sutra, which he worships. All join together in the unity and oneness of prayer.

CHORUS.   Keep your heart without confusion
PRINCESS.   Do not go astray
CHORUS.   Do not go astray
PRINCESS.   The strength of ten voices
CHORUS.   Will rise from your one voice in prayer.
              Gracious Amida![11]

The vision reaches its climax, then fades as the priests awaken from their dream of bliss just as, with another image of travel, the play ends.

PRIESTS.   In the waning night the bell sounds
              And the bell sounds echo
              With the voices crying,
              "Praise to Amida!"
              As we venerate the Buddha
              And hear his miraculous word,
              His holy truthful teaching
              Shines down to light the world:
              In all ten directions
              Mankind finds welcome from him
              As they travel
              In the boat of the True Law.

The oars are used in moving water,
And yet
In the time it takes to push away an oar
The dream of this short night fades
And dawn comes,
Faintly.[12]

Now the priests are becoming reabsorbed into the real world; their spiritual pilgrimage is ending, and their physical one will now begin again; they will return to their familiar existence enlightened. *Taema* seems a perfect artistic representation of Turner's scheme, in which each layer reinforces the others. All participants, the princess, the nun and the girl, the priests, and, presumably, the audience as well, are seeking an authentic pilgrimage experience; all search out paradise, and the play seems a poetic representation of a vast prayer into which the audience seeks to be drawn. The style of the play is perfectly suited to the theme, rising as it does to the first poetic climax, dropping back for the interlude, then moving up to the final poetic heights. All aspects of the presentational *nō* performance—dancing, poetry, masks, and music—help involve the audience in this symbolic act.

My second example is from the world of *jōruri,* specifically a play by Chikamatsu Monzaemon (1653–1724) that has been widely performed both by puppets and by *kabuki* actors. By this time in Japanese history, the theatre, as in Europe, was responding to the rapid development of a bourgeois society; the playwright thus provides a secular view of the pilgrimage progress. The audience now moves toward the role of observer rather than that of participant.

By the time of Chikamatsu, the medieval unities had broken down. The audience for the puppet theatre now constituted a class audience, made up largely of urban merchants who wished for their entertainment a chance to see their own values reflected on the stage, particularly in the so-called *sewamono,* or "domestic dramas," based on contemporary events, where the moral tensions of their own society could be portrayed.

Some insights recorded in Arnold Hauser's *Social History of Art,* although dealing with the European situation during the eighteenth century, suggest both a parallel development with the Japanese cultural situation and an occasional striking similarity. His remarks thus

provide some useful insight into the interactions between Chikamatsu and his audiences. Hauser remarks that a self-consciousness of
social class helps define and limit the work of the playwright at the
time. "The assumption is that the spectator is able to escape from the
influence of the play much less easily when he sees his own class
portrayed on the stage, which he must acknowledge to be his own
class if he is logical, than when he merely sees his own personal character portrayed, which he is free to disown if he wants to."[13]

Hauser goes on to say that the characters in European plays of this
period often become functions of their environment. Men are posited
as social beings, and, "deprived of all autonomy, lose to some extent
the responsibility for their actions." His observations on the effect of
a growing consciousness of a class structure would seem a useful
means to examine a Japanese example, Chikamatsu's *Shinjū ten no
Amijima* (The Love Suicides at Amijima), written in 1721 and often
regarded as Chikamatsu's masterpiece. The play was originally composed for the puppet theatre but its evocative settings and realistic
dialogue, and a plot presumably based on a real love suicide, have
made it a favorite with *kabuki* actors as well.

The plot of the play is simple and like many of the other familiar
"domestic dramas" of Chikamatsu. Jihei, a paper merchant, is in
love with a courtesan, Koharu, despite the real affection felt for him
by his long-suffering wife, Osan. Osan's love for Jihei is such that,
suspecting that the pair may attempt to commit suicide together, she
attempts to avoid the worst by helping her husband ransom Koharu
from the teahouse where she has been forced to serve as an enter-
tainer. The story as it evolves is crafted with a number of effective
confrontations between the characters concerning the nature of love,
duty, honor, and so forth. In this, Magoemon, Jihei's brother, plays a
particularly effective part, serving to some extent the role of the *hon-
nête homme* of Molière as he seeks to bring his brother to the path of
reason and the consolations of social duty. Eventually these tensions
push Koharu and Jihei to suicide. The last two scenes of the play
form a lyrical pilgrimage not to an immediate transcendence, as in
Taema, but to a *communitas* through death. The change in tonality is
immediately obvious; the realistic and often spirited exchanges of the
early scenes that make up the bulk of the play vanish and the language of the text becomes lyrical, indeed highly poetic. This change
of tonality is so striking in the last sequence, and the values the play-

wright propounds there are so different from those expressed in the
rest of the play, that the interpretation of the drama as a pilgrimage
seems virtually the only means to link the two sections of the text
together, at least in terms of the language involved.

In this regard, Turner's conditions again seem to be fulfilled in this
final scene. The lovers, Koharu and Jihei, choose to die together.
Their decision is voluntary. In fact, they have made the decision to
die together early in the play; their real problem, then, concerns how
to carry out their vow. During their pilgrimage to death, they also
choose a special place, out of the way of normal human traffic. They
leave their familiar surroundings and take a fanciful journey, the
stage *michiyuki* so familiar in all forms of the traditional Japanese theatre. Their destination is Amijima (which might be rendered into
English as "Island of Nets"), and on the way they pass by various
islands and bridges that are assigned poetic, often transcendental
meanings as they approach the final spot chosen for their death.

JIHEI.   Look, there is Oe Bridge. We follow the river from Little
           Naniwa Bridge to Funairi Bridge. The farther we jour-
           ney, the closer we approach the road to death.[14]

When they approach the site where they will kill themselves, the
imagery of the play becomes more and more religious.

JIHEI.   Listen—the voices of the temple bells begin to boom.
           How much farther can we go on this way? We are not
           fated to live any longer—let us make an end quickly.
NARRATOR. Tears are strung with the 108 beads of the rosaries in
           their hands. They have come now to Amijima, to the
           Daichō temple; the overflowing sluice gate of a little
           stream beside a bamboo thicket will be their place of
           death.[15]

Finally, time expands as the couple travels their "long last night,"
as they call it. As in *Taema,* the drama ends as the dawn breaks, but
the circumstances are very different. The *communitas* achieved is one
of death. Koharu herself sees her voyage, her pilgrimage, as a means
to salvation.

KOHARU.   What have we to grieve about? Though in this world we
           could not stay together, in the next and through each
           successive world to come until the end of time we shall
           be husband and wife. Every summer for my devotions I
           have copied the All Compassionate and All Merciful
           chapter of the Lotus Sutra, in the hope that we may be
           born on one lotus.[16]

Here at the moment of their deaths, Koharu and Jihei abandon
their normal secular social roles and consciously take on the persona
of pilgrims.

NARRATOR. Jihei whips out his dirk and slashes off his black locks at
           the base of the top knot.
JIHEI.   Look, Koharu. As long as I had this hair, I was Kamiya
           Jihei, Osan's husband, but cutting it has made me a
           monk. I have fled the burning house of the three worlds
           of delusion; I am a priest unencumbered by wife, chil-
           dren, or worldly possessions. Now that I no longer have
           a wife named Osan, you owe her no obligations either.

NARRATOR. In tears he flings away the hair.
KOHARU.   I am happy.
NARRATOR. Koharu takes up the dirk and ruthlessly, unhesitatingly,
           slices through her flowing Shimada coiffure. She casts
           aside the tresses she has so often washed and combed
           and stroked. How heartbreaking to see their locks tan-
           gled with the weeds and midnight frost of this desolate
           field!
JIHEI.   We have escaped the inconstant world, a nun and a
           priest. Our duties as husband and wife belong to our
           profane past.[17]

As in *Taema* the pilgrims pray to Amida.

JIHEI.   You musn't let worries over trifles disturb the prayers of
           your last moments. Keep your eyes on the westward-
           moving moon, and worship it as Amida himself. Con-
           centrate your thoughts on the Western Paradise.[18]

In her ecstasy Koharu now leads Jihei to the final act.

NARRATOR. She smiles. His hands, numbed by the frost, tremble
          before the pale vision of her face, and his eyes are first to
          cloud. He is weeping so profusely that he cannot control
          the blade.
KOHARU.   Compose yourself, but quick!
NARRATOR. Her encouragement lends him strength; the invocations
          to Amida carried by the wind urge a final prayer. Namu
          Amida Butsu. He thrusts in the saving sword.[19]

The combination of images employed by Chikamatsu provides a
striking example of how one set of images, those borrowed from the
kind of religious terminology so highly developed in the medieval *nō,*
can now be employed in a self-consciously artistic way in order to
create a secular, exteriorized version of a similar religious vision.
Artistically, at least, Chikamatsu does believe in his lovers and wants
the audience to do so as well. As Jihei kills himself, he calls out,
"May we be born on one lotus: Hail Amida Buddha!" And indeed,
the last lines in the play suggest that the lovers did earn in death the
transcendence they sought.

NARRATOR. The tale was spread from mouth to mouth. People say
          that they who were caught in the net of Buddha's vow
          immediately gained salvation and deliverance, and all
          who hear the tale of the Love Suicides at Amijima are
          moved to tears.[20]

There is here an effective pun on the word *ami,* which serves both
as the name of the place where the lovers died (Amijima, "Island of
ami, or Nets"), and as a reference to a traditional saying that the nets
of the Buddha are woven meshes able to catch and take up to heaven
the most recalcitrant sinner. Chikamatsu's title thus carries the suggestion of a transcendental message.

In the case of Chikamatsu's drama, then, a play that is realistic in
most of its details ends with a poetic and religious conclusion which,
if not altogether out of keeping with the opening scenes, is certainly
scarcely anticipated in them. The audience is taken by the playwright on a journey, but, unlike the voyage of the priests in *Taema,*

this trip is really an interior one, moving from exterior action to interior motivation, which is expressed poetically. Chikamatsu's technique in creating this movement is accomplished through his skillful use of the narrator. The characters themselves are never required to speak in a fashion out of keeping with their social milieu, or in a fashion so poetic that the verisimilitude that Chikamatsu sought, that famous "slender margin between the real and the unreal" for which he was famous, is never destroyed; rather, the narrator takes over the task of providing a philosophic and poetic gloss on the actions witnessed on the stage. As his role grows larger, the language of the play expands. In this regard Chikamatsu's use of the narrator provides an ingenious solution to the difficulty of how to put poetic dignity in the mouth of everyman, a stylistic problem that has troubled many modern playwrights. Arthur Miller, for example, in *A View from the Bridge,* was driven to adopt, rather awkwardly, the same sort of device in order to lift his text up to the level of eloquence he sought.

Chikamatsu's lovers may commit suicide together in a kind of triumphant search for *communitas,* but they are themselves no larger than life, no Tristan and Isolde. A case might be made that Wagner's orchestra is his narrator, glossing the words of his characters with a high pitch of emotion, but a reading of the text alone of Isolde's love-death shows that the words themselves are conflated far beyond anything that Chikamatsu would have considered appropriate to a human scale. After all, he was writing in his *sewamono* about contemporary figures, not medieval knights, and for many modern readers of the plays, the figures he creates are more passive than active, more acted upon than acted. They are, perhaps, barely heroic enough.

The same phenomenon has been observed in Western drama of the eighteenth and nineteenth centuries, when plays began to be written for middle-class audiences, whose beliefs and assumptions began to show marked differences with those of other levels of society. Here is Georg Lukàcs' description of the hero of such Western bourgeois drama.

> The heroes of the new drama—in comparison to the old—are more passive than active; they are acted upon more than they act for themselves; they defend rather than attack; their heroism is mostly a heroism of anguish, of despair, not bold aggressiveness. Since so much of the inner man has fallen prey to destiny, the last battle is to be enacted

within. The greater the determining force of external factors, the more the center of the tragic conflict is drawn inwards; it becomes internalized, more exclusively a conflict of the spirit.[21]

In the case of Chikamatsu, that anguish is transcended through death, which gives Jihei and Koharu their final dignity. In the composition of this play, as in most of his domestic dramas, Chikamatsu was working with a series of givens, the actual accounts of the lives and deaths of the characters he wished to show on the stage. The remarks of Lukàcs suggest that one means to observe the dramatic movement of the characters in Chikamatsu is to follow the progress of their pilgrimage, their voyage out of their class, out of their problems, and, of course, out of the world altogether, where no final solutions are possible. Again, Lukàcs provides striking insights. "The heroes of the new drama always partake of the ecstatic; they seem to have become conscious of a sense that death can vouchsafe them the transcendence, greatness, and illumination which life withheld, and together with this, a sense that death will fulfill and perfect their personalities."[22]

The townspeople for whom Chikamatsu chose to write could certainly appreciate the poetry of this pilgrimage, framed as it was in terms of the conceptions that made up their own consciousness; they might not carry out such an adventure themselves, but there was a satisfaction for them in watching those whose lives served as witness to the fact that heroism was possible. *The Love Suicides at Amijima* was a large, distorting mirror held up to amplify and dignify the lives of those who came to the theatre. The very movement in the language of the play from prose to poetry confirmed the possibility of that beauty.

If Chikamatsu's play can be seen as a secularizing vision of pilgrimage in a changing Japanese society, then in the contemporary secular world, the modern Japanese theatre can offer up as few sacramental occasions as can its Western counterparts. The audience for contemporary theatre in Japan is young, urban, highly educated, and wholly secular, an audience of intelligentsia that constitutes another kind of "class" altogether. Their interest in religion ranges from indifference to skepticism. In that climate, what forms will drama take, particularly when there has been so much influence from Western theatrical forms and ideals admired and absorbed into the assumptions of the postwar dramatists? Is pilgrimage still possible? Some examples, in fact, would suggest that it is, and that, further, the continuation of such themes argues for some fundamental qualities in the art of the Japanese theatre.

The theme of pilgrimage, in its modern guise, is particularly apparent in a work by the contemporary dramatist Yamazaki Masakazu (born 1934). *Sanetomo shuppan,* written in 1974, was successfully performed in Tokyo, and the author chose it for translation and production in the United States. When preparing the translation, I became aware of just how the mental constructs of the pilgrimage mentality were present, almost as unspoken assumptions, in the text. The conception of the drama itself is quite sophisticated and in a sense repeats the structures of Chikamatsu and of *Taema,* where actual locations, events, and characters are placed on the stage. In this case, Yamazaki chose the figure of Minamoto Sanetomo (1182–1219), the young shogun of Japan who was installed after the Heike wars that ended in 1185; a gifted poet and a remarkable statesman, his assassination marked a tragic turning point in the fortunes of the Kamakura shogunate. Sanetomo's character has long fascinated writers, scholars, and thinkers, and Yamazaki has made this fascination part of the construct of his play by superimposing the figure of Hamlet onto that of Sanetomo, in which the same search for truth and the same questions of the significance of existence come to the fore as the protagonist questions all the assumptions of the life he finds around him. Yamazaki has constructed the text as a kind of psychodrama assembled by those who knew him—his mother, uncle, relatives, allies, enemies; they are presented as ghosts who reconstruct and examine various incidents in Sanetomo's life. Much of the central section of the play concerns the young shogun's desire to build a ship to sail to China. As the incidents concerning this event are reconstructed, discussed, relived on the stage, Yamazaki makes use of an expanded poetic time that puts his drama into the expanded psychological atmosphere redolent of the atmosphere of pilgrimage that Turner described. In this regard, Yamazaki's use of the dichotomies of the stage versus reality, acting versus living, memory versus action, effectively combine to reveal his central concerns. As with Chikamatsu, the central events presented by Yamazaki are well known to his audience; both dramatists play on what the audience already understands so as to move them to a higher and different level of understanding and empathy.

The full title of the play, translated into English, is *Sanetomo Sets Sail,* and the events of the play suggest on one level a wholly secular end to the theme of pilgrimage, for the ship never leaves Japan. Sanetomo's sole desire is to go to China, his own idea of a cultural paradise, but his vessel is built without sufficient knowledge of seagoing sail craft and never leaves the beach. Each character in the play has formed a different idea of why Sanetomo wants to go to China, and each of these convictions in turn is based on the differing motives, obsessions, and blindnesses of the particular character who devises them. Does Sanetomo know himself? Early in the play he attempts to articulate to the ghost of his dead father some of his feelings in a scene that comes closest to Yamazaki's chosen model of *Hamlet.*

SANETOMO.   Show me your face . . . I want to tell you something. I want you to do something for me. Speak. I have the force. And the strength of will. And too much curiosity. I'll do anything, try anything. Risk some adventure? Where should I go? Speak. Tell me. Am I to live? To die?[23]

Despite the mistrust of all those who surround him, Sanetomo makes a decision to build the ship, to prepare his men. His powerful uncle Yoshitoki, who admires and loves his nephew, now becomes convinced that Sanetomo has some sort of transcendental purpose in mind, some purpose which he, Yoshitoki, because of his own view of the world and its scheming politics, cannot understand. Convinced of this, Yoshitoki now sets out to try to grasp in his own terms the seemingly ambiguous purposes of Sanetomo's effort. The huge ship is finally completed, but Sanetomo's Chinese shipwright adviser remains concerned about the impracticality of the voyage.

CHEN.   I do not know. I do not. Do you really intend to go on board? Do you plan to board her and sail across the sea?

SANETOMO.   What a nuisance you are. Of course.

CHEN.   But you must not. It is not a ship. It is an apparition. A ship of two thousand stone. What is more, you had three cabins built. The prow of the ship is too heavy. Too dangerous. And the weights in the bottom have increased three times over. That is bad. So unreason-

able. Sailing a ship like that you will sink, even on a fair
day. Please. Sanetomo. Listen to what I tell you.

SANETOMO. To sink . . . or not to sink . . . sink . . . not to sink
. . .[24]

Is Sanetomo's scheme dream or reality? Yoshitoki thinks in the end
that he has come to understand his nephew's motivations. He recites
to his sister Masako, the young shogun's mother, a poem by Sanetomo.

YOSHITOKI. "The world itself
 Is but a reflection in a mirror:
 If it seems to be there, it is;
 If not, then there is nothing."
I'm not quite sure I understand the part about being
there and not being there. But if the whole world is just
a reflection, then where does that leave us, my dear sister? If Kamakura, the Emperor himself, everything is
an illusion, then all my strength evaporates. And more
awesome is the man who can go on existing, serene,
knowing that everything is an illusion. A man who con-
ducts his life with good sense, and without despair, even
though nothing, nothing at all makes any difference.
With such a strong man nearby, I am overwhelmed. I
lose the strength to go on living.

MASAKO. Calm yourself, Yoshitoki. You are overanxious. You are
tired.

YOSHITOKI. Now I have only one hope. It is Sanetomo's ship.
Because this is the only time he has positively opposed
me. The one time he has stepped off the path I have
prepared for him. And with such passion. Masako. We
will allow him to do it. I want to see it. I want to see him
once, firm in the belief that this world is not merely an
illusion.[25]

Sanetomo prepares his ship, but the vessel is too large and is destroyed at the launching on the beach. Sanetomo now gives up his
transcendental voyage and makes plans instead for a this-worldly

political voyage, to become a courtier and a poet. Even those who are shortly to murder him cannot understand his change in motivation.

The play concludes with a scene in which his wife asks all those who knew him to enact an incident that never occurred in life, the moment when Sanetomo would actually set sail. It is his murderer, his nephew Kugyō, who, now watching the sails unfurl at last, comes closest to grasping the meaning of Sanetomo's gesture.

KUGYŌ. I'm overwhelmed. He's really putting all he's got into it. In the middle of a senseless dream, when he knows nothing will come of it, why does he never become discouraged? Why?[26]

Sanetomo, it seems, has made his interior and transcendental voyage after all.

Yamazaki's play was written in the kind of climate that exists in the postwar theatre movement around the world. His dialogue is realistic and psychologically attuned to the changing inner self-perceptions of the characters. Yet the play's purposes do not stop there; indeed they are intended to lead contemporary spectators from a sterile emphasis on individual motive and obsession to a larger vision of the universe, a world where personal predilections dissolve in a movement toward a larger gathering together. The whole structure of the play is calculated to permit the spectators to transcend the world of those who surround Sanetomo, with their plots and schemes, and rise up with him onto the platform of the ship. In the pattern of the medieval *nō*, the person seeking enlightenment went on a pilgrimage himself; now Yamazaki combines the idea of physical pilgrimage, appropriate to the historical Sanetomo, with the image of an internal search for transcendence, so much a part of the way in which contemporary human beings conceptualize the possibilities of understanding life today. If this represents a bonding between Freud and the Buddha, then it must be said that, in theatrical terms at least, they have more in common than might have been supposed.

All three of these plays, then, and the traditions they represent show a poetic style, a thrust away from mimesis, an invitation for the audiences to lose themselves in an experience that can draw them out of their normal mental structures of reality. Metaphysical melodrama turns out to have a logic all of its own. In that regard, the three examples provided here were not chosen with an eye to validating Turner's pilgrimage model; rather, Turner's insights can help illustrate this powerful pattern of a poetic desire for oneness which began with the *nō* and continues to exist in the secular theatre of today. The movement beyond the abstract logic of words and social data toward a vision of a shared communal world that lies beyond is as strong an impetus behind, say, the avant-garde theatre of Suzuki Tadashi and his *Trojan Women* as it remains behind *Taema*. It is perhaps for such reasons that the so-called post-modern theatre of Suzuki and his contemporaries has gone back to the roots of the Japanese dramatic experience to come forth and reassert the genius of the Japanese theatre, not in the realm of a Chekhov, an Ibsen, or a Molière, however much has been learned from them, but from a transcendental thrust that, in our culture, has perhaps only been fully visible in the best of modern dance. What Zeami and Chikamatsu knew, and what Claudel, Yeats, and Britten recognized, is finally coming to be appreciated again in contemporary Japan. It is to such new theatre, rather than to the Brecht and Molière that I saw in the 1950s, that spectators around the world are beginning to look with excitement and enormous admiration. The pilgrimage, happily, would seem to continue.

6

The Pilgrimage of Personality
Kamo no Chōmei and Cultural Continuity, an Example from the *Nō*

IN HIS book on the nature of modern culture, *The Triumph of the Therapeutic,* Philip Rieff reminds us that "as cultures change, so do the modal types of personalities that are their bearers."[1] Rieff has chosen Freud as the modal type of personality for the twentieth century and goes on to suggest that in any culture the perceived personality, not the abstract idea, remains the essential element in which a society can recognize itself. "In culture," he writes, "it is always the example that survives; the person is the essential idea."[2] Any adjustment in what he calls the "common and implicitly understood" beliefs of a particular historical moment will therefore cause a shift in the perceived nature of the figure who has gained such an essential status in the history of the culture.

Looking at medieval Japanese culture, Kamo no Chōmei (1153–1216) may represent an excellent example of a "modal personality" who so appears to typify certain attitudes of his period that he is often chosen to represent them. Yet in the centuries since Chōmei first became accepted as such a figure, the historical and psychological truths he represented have been continually adjusted. As Japanese culture added new values and reconstituted old ones, perceptions about the character of the cultural figures employed shifted accordingly; models, such as Chōmei, were seldom discarded, but their significance was reinterpreted. Such a situation is familiar enough to readers of literature who continue to find "new" meanings appropriate to their generation in older texts. But in this case, when a text in turn is taken to represent the literary record of an actual life, as in the *Hōjōki* (An Account of My Hut), one of the best-loved and studied texts in classical Japanese literature, then additional considerations arise.

One example of the cultural rearrangements made possible in relation to Chōmei's historical life can be seen in the *nō* drama entitled *Kamo no Chōmei,* in which Chōmei himself appears as the *shite,* or central character. The play itself no longer remains in the contemporary *nō* repertory but the text appeared in several well-known collections printed in the early years of this century. As with many *nō* dramas, the exact date and authorship of the text remain unclear. A tentative estimate, based on internal evidence, would place the composition of the text between 1500 and 1650, thus providing a late medieval view of Chōmei and, by extension, of the author's conception of the social and literary function of the real and the symbolic role of a recluse. The *Hōjōki,* written in 1212, provides the source material for the play and for the images of Chōmei presented, but an examination of that earlier work reveals that a number of striking changes in detail have been made since the thirteenth century.

The play can briefly be described as follows. The play opens with the entrance of the *waki,* or chief subsidiary character, and his companion. They have come from Kyoto to see the cherry blossoms at Mount Hino, southeast of Kyoto on the hills near the Uji River, close to the spot where Chōmei was said to have built his celebrated hut. We are not told during what period the play takes place. The presumption, however, is that Chōmei is already dead and so appears to the priests as an apparition.

With appropriate elegance, the visitors quote a poem from the imperial poetry anthology, the *Goshūishū* (1075), to indicate their enthusiasm for the blossoms.

> Although we see them every spring
> We never tire of them, the blossoms;
> As years pass, they bloom
> Ever more luxuriantly.[3]

When they arrive at the spot they seek, they notice a small hut and begin to wonder if indeed it might be the one built by Chōmei when he left the capital to become a Buddhist recluse. Their speculation ends when the *shite,* Chōmei himself, appears, chanting the familiar opening lines of the *Hōjōki:* "The flow of the river is ceaseless and its water is never the same. The bubbles that float in the pools, now vanishing, now forming, are not of long duration. . . ."[4]

The visitors ask if they might rest in the hut, but Chōmei reminds them that the space is too small to accommodate them; after all, he says, paraphrasing the end of the *Hōjōki,* he is not a mystic sage like the Indian Vimalakirti, the Buddhist saint who could create in his hut a space for thirty-two thousand lion thrones; he is a mere hermit who has no magic power. Be that as it may, his visitors reply, all can seek salvation. Hearing this, Chōmei allows them to enter "the matchless gate" of the Buddhist law. In this rarefied atmosphere, the visitors remark on the beauty of the blossoms, which, in the spring wind, seem to scatter like snow, as though a heavenly being were strewing flowers before the Buddha.

The two then ask Chōmei to tell them his story. This request triggers a lengthy passage that represents the central portion of the text of the play. Chōmei provides a long recitation, occasionally punctuated by the chorus, in which he tells of his trials and tribulations in the world, as recorded in the *Hōjōki.* The long speech is an amalgam of bits of that earlier text; they record various historical happenings, the great fire in 1177, the moving of the capital, the famine in 1181, and the earthquake in 1185. All these unhappy incidents, says Chōmei, represent the kind of disasters that made him recognize the evanescence of the world.

Until this point in the text the play has presented merely an elegant and rather straightforward dramatization of the original material contained in the *Hōjōki.* Now, suddenly, the play takes a different turn. The visitors tell Chōmei that he must be weary after such a long recitation, and they ask his servant, a youth, played by a *kokata,* or child performer, to serve the hermit some sake. In the original *Hōjōki,* of course, Chōmei has no server, although he does mention going for an occasional walk with a boy. The older text reads: "At the foot of the mountain is a rough-hewn cottage where the guardian of the mountain lives. He has a son who sometimes comes to visit me. When I am bored with whatever I am doing, I often go for a walk with him as my companion. He is ten, and I am sixty; though our ages differ greatly, we take pleasure in each other's company."[5] In the *nō* version, however, the boy seems to function directly as a servant and as a disciple of Chōmei, now elevated to the role of a sage.

The boy serves rice wine to the three, and the visitor, paraphrasing Po chü-i, the Chinese T'ang-dynasty poet so admired in Japan, remarks that a good drink in this life may be just as valuable as a good

name in history. Chōmei agrees, and he reminds his new friends of
the legend of "The Three Laughers of Tiger Ravine," an incident
from Chinese cultural lore also popular in Japan. On Mount Lu,
says Chōmei, the Buddhist sage Hui-yüan secluded himself and
would not go into the world beyond Tiger Ravine. The poet T'ao
Yüan-ming and the Taoist adept Lu Hsiu-ching, taking a barrel of
wine, went to the valley. Therefore, Chōmei reminds his visitors,
drinking wine may go against the teachings of the Buddha, yet he
who has never found himself moved by the experience of doing so is
less than a beast. Chōmei then goes on to recount how the three,
happy to drink and talk together, unwittingly wandered past the
boundary of Hui-yüan's self-enforced place of retirement.

With these Chinese references and citations, Chōmei's role as a
hermit appears to take on additional dimensions. In order to specu-
late on the possible cultural significance of these additions to the Chōmei legend, it is necessary to give some background on this story of
Hui-yüan which Chōmei recounts and with which he identifies himself. No mention of the incident, of course, appears in the original
Hōjōki. The link is made by the author of the *nō* play.

All three figures in the story are actual historical personages,
although this incident concerning them is doubtless apocryphal. Hui-
yüan (344–416) was a convert to Buddhism who retired to Mount Lu,
south of the Yangtze River, where he built himself a hermitage in the
mountains. A figure of great importance in his own generation, he
was visited by many but vowed never to leave his surroundings.
Tiger Ravine was the farthest spot from his hermitage to which he
would go in seeing off his guests. On one occasion, when he was visited by the great poet T'ao Yüan-ming (365–427) and the Taoist Lu
Hsiu-ching (406–477), the three fell into such a harmonious conversation that they walked too far. Realizing what had happened, the three
burst into laughter, thus suggesting the title given to the incident,
"The Three Laughers of Tiger Ravine." The anecdote appeared in a
number of Chinese literary accounts and became the subject of Buddhist ink paintings both in China and in Japan. Chōmei's reference,
therefore, is by no means an obscure one. In an article on this legend
and its importance in the history of Japanese culture, John Rosenfield indicates that paintings on the subject (including one inscribed
with a poem by the great Sung-dynasty poet Su Tung-p'o) were well
known in China by the latter half of the eleventh century.[6] The con-

tinued popularity of the subject indicates that the real significance of "The Three Laughers" in China goes beyond the charm of the incident itself. Rather, the harmony of the three is a symbolic, artistic representation of the "unity of the three creeds," Buddhism (Hui-yüan), Confucianism (T'ao Yüan-ming), and Taoism (Lu Hsiu-ching). The close friendship of the three served as a means to point out that a "higher truth" bound all the religions of China together.

As Rosenfield points out, the incident of "The Three Laughers" was known in Japan by the Kamakura period and continued to inspire paintings through the Tokugawa period, notably in a particularly elegant screen on the subject painted by Ike no Taiga about 1750. The iconography of the paintings in both Chinese and Japanese culture seems roughly the same. Incidentally, Rosenfield indicates that in these paintings there is often a servant boy looking on as the laughers walk, which may explain the appearance of Chōmei's servant in the play. The synthesis of the three creeds, however, evidently did not pose the philosophical problems in Japan that it did in China. Japanese artists therefore tended to use the anecdote in a more general way. Nor were representations of the legend limited to painting. There were poems that referred to the story, and there is a *nō* play entitled *Sanshō* (Three Smiles) in which the incident is directly enacted on the stage. This play, which remains in the modern repertory, has, like the *nō* text under discussion here, not been identified as to author. The first record of a performance of *Sanshō* was in 1596, which suggests the persistent fascination that the legend held in Japanese cultural history.

In the play *Kamo no Chōmei*, Chōmei seems to identify himself with Hui-yüan: he says that he will drink with his visitors just as Hui-yüan did, a detail, incidentally, not mentioned in any version of the original legend that I have been able to uncover. Characters in *nō* dramas often show various layers of their personalities during the course of a play. The contemporary Japanese dramatist Yamazaki Masakazu has stressed this important principle in the *nō:* "In the dramatic pattern, one protagonist bears two identities, and the contrast between these two identities provides a powerful theatrical effectiveness."[7] In just such a fashion, Chōmei and his visitors transform themselves momentarily into Chinese sages, giving a depth and resonance to the scene impossible without such a metamorphosis. Such a transformation not only permits the dramatist to link Chōmei to an

earlier religious figure of great potency, but, on a more practical
level, provides him with the means to introduce the final dance scene
requisite to any *nō* performance. Chōmei and the chorus alternate in
telling the story of how the three laughers drank and so passed the
ravine, without mentioning the metaphysical conversations so important in the Chinese context of the original legend. This reenact-
ment by Chōmei and his companions of the Chinese paradigm
makes them in turn serve as a living link in a larger tradition, of
which they now become exemplars.

In the final section of the play the chorus comments, in a burst of
patriotism, that while the Chinese sages drank a muddy liquor, Chōmei and his friends have sparkling sake. The youth, quoting still
another poem from the *Goshūishū* on the beauty of the cherries, fills
their glasses and dances for the three. Eventually the visitors remind
themselves that the party must end; Chōmei, paraphrasing the
Hōjōki for the final time, says that "this hut may take after that of
Vimalakirti, but I do not uphold the law as well as did Panthaka, the
most foolish of the Buddha's disciples." The two visitors murmur a
Buddhist prayer and depart. Chōmei, alone, looks at the sky and
recites the poem traditionally attached to the end of the text of the
Hōjōki, although, according to modern scholars, it was probably not
written by Chōmei himself.

> How painful to have seen
> The moonlight vanish
> Beyond the rim of the hill;
> Yet how wonderful it would be to see
> The light [of the Buddha] that never
>   fades.[8]

So ends the text.

The author of the play, and, by extension, the spectators who
watched it, seemed content to give the historical Chōmei, through his
own eloquence and his identification in the play with the great sages
of China, a high status both in religious and in cultural terms. In the
actual *Hōjōki,* of course, Chōmei makes a number of deprecating
remarks about his own state of enlightenment. "Why should I thus
drone on about myself? The essence of the Buddha's teaching to man
is that we must not have attachment to any object. It is a sin for me

now to love my little hut, and my attachment to its solitude may also be a hindrance to salvation. Why should I waste any more precious time in relating to such trifling pleasures?"[9]

Such remarks are appealing to a modern reader for their ironic candor. In the play, however, such self-irony is subsumed in a larger transcendental image of the wise and beneficent sage who can occasionally share companionship in this world while remaining outside it. Chōmei's ironies, as it were, disappear in the depths of Hui-yüan's laughter. And the dramatist, by this addition of a dimension not in the original account, has allowed the historical character of Chōmei to shift in its definition accordingly.

This particular religious view of Chōmei is not necessarily emphasized by all those who have continued to summon up his image from the past. A number of later writers have stressed his literary rather than his religious proclivities. The Tokugawa *haiku* poet Matsuo Bashō, for example, in his *Oi no kobumi* (Records of a Travel-worn Satchel) pays homage to Chōmei as a profound figure in the Japanese cultural tradition and cites him as one who brought the form of the travel diary to perfection. The great modern poet Nishiwaki Junzaburō sees Chōmei as the creator of the Japanese pastoral. For Nishiwaki, Chōmei's art is far more important than his religion, as Nishiwaki explains in his own quaint and evocative English.

> During his pastoral life in the cool valley of Kamo his idea might well be compared to *un epi de blé,* and his heart to the heath-bell. But what of his hope to live in art and of his new mode of thought? Well, his art only ripened into maudlin Hinduism, which compelled him to prefer religion to art; and his own doctrine of change was easily absorbed up in Buddhism, indeed. Buddhism really had baulked his own way to the kingdom of real artists and to the realm of philosophy or wisdom. For this single reason, even, I for one have a grudge against Buddhism.[10]

For Nishiwaki, Chōmei's triumph lies in his art.

> His sentimentality is nothing but religious, yet he always found a beauty of the most artistic sort in the very withering of human life, no less than in that of flower or beast. . . . Yet he was a serene lover of beauty; in that prior's diary he says that he is much like a cloud itself, adrift at the mercy of Destiny or Death; but adding that *a desire for a longer life will revive when I see beautiful landscapes.*[11]

The cultural significance of Chōmei's personality, then, seems to depend on the period and on the person who summons him up. Nevertheless, certain strong lines of continuity run through all the variations on the Chōmei legend. This continuity, it seems to me, has chiefly to do with the surprisingly personal self-awareness that Chōmei shows in discussing his own reactions to the world in which he lives, in order to tacitly posit a series of definitions about the nature of his own self. The cunning mixture of observation, reflection, abstraction, and self-revelation in the *Hōjōki* have caught, in one way or another, the attention of every generation that has read and studied it.

Yet those successive generations have, as I have hoped to suggest here, nevertheless defined that continuity in a slightly different way. For the writer of the *nō* play, that "laugh" of self-awareness added through the reference to Hui-yüan best summed up the essential element that the author sought to locate in Chōmei's "modal" personality. Chōmei's skill at providing self-revelation explicated in the context of a careful literary framework, and his ability to mix high style with guarded personal confession remain appealing in modern times, and to foreign readers as well as to Japanese. If Philip Rieff is correct in suggesting that contemporary Western insights have been developed in a Freudian age, then it is no wonder that we are drawn to the personality of Chōmei, who conceals as he reveals. We try to search his writings, as we try to search in ourselves, in order to posit what the true nature of Chōmei's vivid yet elusive personality might be.

The play *Kamo no Chōmei,* then, represents one stage in a continuous process undertaken by various Japanese writers and thinkers in order to understand and reevaluate a central personality in Japanese culture. In this case at least, an examination of any particular stage of that process might reveal as much about the preconceptions and interests of those various interpreters as it does about the appealing, complex, and many-faceted model under scrutiny.

III

PRESENT TO PAST
TO PRESENT

7

Mori Ōgai and Jean-Paul Sartre
Some Intersections of Biography, History, and Literature

WHATEVER the genre involved, history, biography, or fiction, human beings, and their varied responses to the life that surrounds them, remain at the center. In that regard the second sentence of the preface of Jean-Paul Sartre's *L'Idiot de la famille* (The Family Idiot), published in 1971 and his last major work, poses a crucial question for all three: "What, at this point in time, can we know about a man?" Sartre then goes on. "It seemed to me that this question could only be answered by studying a specific case. What do we know, for example, about Gustave Flaubert?"[1] The question seems a straightforward one, but Sartre required more than a thousand pages to attempt an answer, and the work remained unfinished at his death. Sartre was trying, in his attempt to articulate the connections between individual human consciousness and a larger historical understanding, to break the traditional literary barriers between the ways of ordering history and imagination, and his work stands as a much-celebrated example of a new and authentic methodology.

Still, Sartre's methods, while sophisticated, are not altogether new. As a scholar interested in Japanese literature, I was struck, in reading *The Family Idiot,* to see how closely the author's strategies parallel those used by Mori Ōgai in his biographical reconstruction of the life of a Tokugawa-period doctor, *Shibue Chūsai,* written in 1916. Ōgai, like Sartre, wishes to reconstruct the life of a man who deeply interests him, and in doing so he creates methods of historical investigation and interpretation that bear a remarkable resemblance to those of his later French counterpart. Ōgai, of course, was a great writer in the modern Japanese tradition, and for many of my Japanese colleagues and friends, *Shibue Chūsai* is his masterpiece; but like

Sartre's study of Flaubert, it fits awkwardly if at all into the normal categories of literature, at least as defined and practiced in the English-speaking world. Reading Sartre, who is so much more explicit in explaining his methodologies, can be of some help in explicating Ōgai's often unarticulated assumptions. One fact is clear at once, however. Each author, in searching out the life of another, finishes by telling an enormous amount about himself; and indeed this sort of autobiographical self-consciousness becomes, in both cases, a crucial part of the basic methodology involved. The hidden question that lies under Sartre's question, "What do we know, for example, about Gustave Flaubert?" thus becomes, "What can we know about ourselves?" The fact that both authors came upon the same means of structuring their inquiries suggests, finally, nothing about mutual influences, but points up instead an inevitable congruence of technique achieved altogether independently by both writers in the course of two similar projects.

What triggers this methodology? In both cases, it seems to me, it is the fact of the continuing presence of history itself. Each writer in his own way was committed to a sense of the individual as defined in terms of the historical moment with which he was inevitably engaged. Interestingly enough, both Sartre and Ōgai spent formative years in Germany, and both took a profound interest in the kind of continental philosophy to which they were exposed there. Both integrated into their own creative work the conviction, perhaps gained by that exposure, that any authentic consciousness that a man can achieve can only come from his sense of the historical flux in which he finds himself and in which he must make his own, personal way. Sartre, in working out his own methodologies to explicate this conviction, made use of certain Marxist concepts; Ōgai, several generations earlier, turned rather to Kant and Vaihinger. Both, however, came to the conviction that only a sense of history and of the movement of ideas, and ideologies, through history can lead a writer to a necessary level of self-consciousness. Such a consciousness, in turn, can allow the writer to find a means to assess the implications, the larger significance of the relativities of the particular subject he has chosen for investigation. Writers such as Sartre and Ōgai, in their maturity of self-understanding, attempted when writing of the past to envision the real nature of their own contemporary societies, but without relinquishing a sense of the limits of their own understanding, precisely because they too knew that they shared in the unspoken assumptions of their own period. In investigating their historical subjects, it thus becomes necessary for them to investigate themselves.

Both *Shibue Chūsai* and *The Family Idiot* were written as case studies of figures who held a tremendous personal attraction to their respective authors. Both authors were in their full maturity when they took up their researches. Sartre was sixty-six when he published the first section of his text; Ōgai was fifty-four. Sartre's manuscript remained unfinished at his death; Ōgai's included 119 separate sections and remained virtually his longest work, apart from a few more strictly historical accounts written a few years later. Both works reveal as well an evolving point of view, since both authors, as they carried out their investigations, shaped and reshaped their responses to what they found as they proceeded. Their responses, their sense of the significance of the life they observed, grew and changed as their knowledge of their subject increased. Both studies are full of questions, and self-questioning.

If these works were, in the ordinary sense of the word, written in the style considered appropriate to one of their components, if they were books of history, of fiction, or of biography, then the methodologies of historical investigation developed by both writers, in which the investigator continues to intrude into his material, seeking out the significance of his discoveries, questioning his readers, and himself, would exceed the accepted canon of stylistic possibilities. Both writers, however, express in their respective texts their conviction that these presumed intrusions represent in fact a crucial part of the process of composition and stand as an equally central element in the kind and quality of understanding each seeks, in his own way, from his readers.

Another commonality between the two works involves a search on the part of both writers for a means to integrate themselves into their subject matter. They have chosen to write of men with whom they can feel a sense of personal identification, a crucial empathy; in one sense they wish to explicate a life that can illumine and justify their own, somewhat in the manner envisioned by the philosopher Wilhelm Dilthey (1833–1911) in his concept of *verstehen* (understanding), an intersubjective understanding between the writer and his subject matter.[2] By seeking Self in Other, the projects chosen by these two writers possess a kind of obsessive significance for them, revealed in a flow from the subjective to the objective and back to the subjective that, allowing for differences of style, can be said to characterize both narratives.

With this much by way of generality, a few remarks about the nature of each text are in order.[3] In the case of Sartre, why did he choose Flaubert? His preface is both eloquent and specific. Sartre lists four reasons. First of all, sufficient documentation exists, in the form of letters, books, articles, and so forth for the purposes of an investigation. Secondly, he feels an intimate and rather complicated relationship with Flaubert. "In 1943, rereading his correspondence . . . I felt I had a score to settle with Flaubert and ought therefore to get to know him better."[4] Thirdly, for Sartre, man is never totally divorced from society, "never an individual; it would be more fitting to call him a *universal singular.*"[5] One means to study the objective human being would therefore require the study of that person's writing, where a deliberate attempt at objectification has been undertaken. An uncritical examination of the flux of the lived life itself cannot yield the same certitude of significance. Lastly, for Sartre, Flaubert is a crucial literary figure, "the creator of the modern novel, [who] stands at the crossroads of all our literary problems today."[6] This nineteenth-century writer, then, has a relevance not only for Sartre but through him, as a modern man and a contemporary writer, to the present generation for whom he has composed his account.

In making his study of Flaubert, Sartre differentiates between what he terms "concepts," abstract ideas that apparently lie outside the relativism of history and reveal a larger objectivity, and "notions," thoughts that "carry time within themselves" and permit a special empathy between the subject under study and the writer. It is on the basis of an examination of such "notions" that Sartre attempts to find correspondences between himself and Flaubert, for, he insists, before one can judge Flaubert, one must know him. Sartre assembles documents, letters, books, memoirs, and he reads, then rereads, slowly creating a close reciprocity between what represents for him the objective situation of culture and literature in France in the nineteenth century and Flaubert's "subjective self," so that, as Sartre puts it in his preface, Flaubert, "summed up and for this reason universalized by his epoch, in turn resumes it by reproducing himself in it as singularity."[7]

Mori Ōgai is less explicit, perhaps more modest in the complexity of his methodologies, which tend to develop in an organic fashion as he continues to move along through his developing narrative structure. Still, the congruence of purpose shown by both writers suggests that Sartre's four reasons for having chosen Flaubert may serve as a useful tool to characterize Ōgai's techniques. In the first place, Ōgai, like Sartre, is convinced that there is sufficient information available in the nineteenth-century Japanese documents to make the re-creation of such a life possible. Indeed, part of the considerable excitement in reading *Shibue Chūsai* comes from experiencing with Ōgai the thrill of the chase, as he seeks out the documents he needs, visiting temples, looking through old records, talking with the descendants of his protagonists, and so forth. Sometimes Ōgai's intuitions as to where to find information prove false. Sometimes his forays produce facts that lead him to different conclusions than those he had first imagined. In this regard Sartre remains more passive, usually remaining in his study. We watch both writers sift through the evidence they find, but Ōgai makes the chronicle of his actual physical search for evidence an integral part of his methodology.

Sartre speaks of a "score to settle with Flaubert," and as a writer finds a close identification, possibly a felt rivalry with his predecessor. Ōgai's relationship with Chūsai is equally complex in that Chūsai was a doctor of traditional Japanese medicine; yet Ōgai, trained in Western medicine and by this point in his career the surgeon general of the Japanese Army, was less a rival than an observer, seeking out hidden parallels between his life and the life of another man whose learning and convictions were considerably different from his. Different, perhaps, but the relationship between Chūsai's intellectual life, sense of place, and philosophical convictions are characterized in such a way by Ōgai that he could come to feel an attraction to "becoming Chūsai."

Sartre's conviction that a man may only be objectified in his writing, that reality lies in the documents left behind more than in the shifting fragments that constitute the lived life, is only partially echoed in the attitudes expressed by Ōgai. In the first place, Ōgai was not dealing with a protagonist who considered himself primarily a writer, although Chūsai did leave a certain amount of poetry and other material, and there were many other relevant documents about his literary interests to be perused as well. Still, the basic nature of the documents available for examination by Sartre and Ōgai differed greatly in some respects. The various strands woven into Ōgai's narrative allow Chūsai's persona to emerge in startling and complex detail, but he seldom turned up materials that permit the kind of view of the inner life that is afforded Sartre through his access to Flaubert. In some ways, too, Ōgai's own personal convictions, doubtless developed from his Confucian heritage, may have sustained him in the view that human beings ultimately objectify themselves by what they do and by how, in the fullest sense, they treat others. These assumptions, plus the nature of the documentation available, gave Ōgai the challenge of reconstructing the complex social web of relationships in which Chūsai found himself. They provided Ōgai as well with the difficulty, which his art surmounts triumphantly, of re-creating the emotional lives of his characters from a smaller and seemingly less rich cache of material, in terms of psychological content.

Finally, just as Sartre found relevance in Flaubert for his own time, so Ōgai sought to find in Chūsai the hidden congruences that lurk below a seeming disruption between past and present in Japan; for Ōgai's contemporaries, Chūsai and his generation inhabited a world whose artifacts, habitudes, and values now seemed to have vanished and so were somehow discredited. Others, like the writer Nagai Kafū, were to point out in their own fiction and essays the ramifications of this change in order to castigate the present; Ōgai, however, sought to identify the subtle connections that linked that past and his present together. From Ōgai's point of view, any real and necessary understanding of the present was impossible to achieve without a consciousness of the past. A synthesis of an understanding of the past and the present, on the other hand, could help lead to a perspective of the future as it unfolds. Like Sartre, Ōgai, as he constructs his lengthy account of Chūsai, develops a methodology of empathy, entering so far inside his characters that he can begin to identify the unspoken assumptions and relationships that linked objective situations of Tokugawa society with the inner world of Chūsai, his remarkable family, and his friends. In answer to Sartre's question, "What can we know about a man?" Ōgai seeks to understand what we, in this century, can learn about a man who seemingly inhabited another world altogether.

Ōgai's search for an active empathy can be observed at the very opening of the book. The first chapter of *Shibue Chūsai* begins as follows:

> Thirty-seven years are as an instant
> With little talent I have extended my medical studies;
> Ruin or success in the world—I leave all to fate
> With a heart truly at peace, poverty and suffering have no meaning.
>
> This is a poem in which Shibue Chūsai expressed his deepest feelings. I imagine it must have been written in the second year of Tempō [1831]. Chūsai at that time was the physician in attendance on Tsugaru Yukitsugu, the lord of the castle at Hirosaki.[8]

Ōgai goes on at some length to analyze the private feelings that he finds hidden in Chūsai's formal poem, written in classical Chinese, creating a whole subtext of emotions, autobiographical revelations, and social relationships. In doing so Ōgai begins to question the assumptions a reader at his time (and such a reader would be closer to our own than to those of Chūsai's time) would bring to these four lines. Did Chūsai really mind being poor, muses Ōgai; what did it mean for a man like Chūsai to seek for the contentment of a life in balance, and what were the terms in which such contentment could or would be couched? What, in short, can we know of a man at this point in time, our point in time?

As Ōgai's text proceeds, he sifts the evidence, weighs each fact, ponders each discovery in terms of the implicit model of a spiritual and social totality that he continues to construct at the same time, using the individual facts he finds to posit a whole, moving back and forth from detail to larger consideration in a manner quite reminiscent of Sartre's technique in *The Family Idiot*.

In chapter 6 of *Shibue Chūsai* there is a passage of considerable beauty that helps suggest Ōgai's whole methodology.

> Chūsai was a physician and a bureaucrat. He studied books of philosophy on various aspects of Confucianism, he read history, and he studied in the field of the arts as well, literature and poetry. In this regard we resemble each other very closely indeed. Still, one noticeable difference is that, putting aside the fact that we lived at different times,

our lives have not had precisely the same value. No, in fact, I must admit there is one enormous difference. Although Chūsai was able to establish himself as a real student in philosophy and in art, I have not been able to escape from my own vague world of the dilettante. Looking at Chūsai, I can only feel a sense of shame.

Chūsai was indeed a man who walked the same road that I have. Yet his stride represented something that I could never hope to imitate. He was vastly superior to me in every way. I owe him all my respect. Indeed, the extraordinary thing is that he walked not only all the great roads but came and went by the byways as well. Not only did he study Neo-Confucianism, but he amused himself with books of heraldry and old maps of Edo. If Chūsai had been my contemporary, our sleeves would surely have rubbed as we walked through those muddy lanes. An intimacy would have developed between us. And I would have come to love him.[9]

Without this empathy, this identification between the author and his material, the kind of synthesis Ōgai was attempting could never have been created. That identification in turn allowed Ōgai, as it did Sartre, to imagine situations, create dialogue, introduce family members, and reconstruct relationships, all in order to situate the object of his study in the daily emotional environment of Chūsai's lived experience. In particular Ōgai lavished an enormous amount of care on his re-creation of Chūsai's wife, Io, and her children; indeed, Chūsai's wife may well represent the most remarkably moving and sympathetic character to emerge from all Ōgai's historical writing, fictional or biographical.[10] Ōgai is anxious as well to link the emotional lives of these persons to the kind of understanding available to his own generation, and he makes them intelligible by moving back and forth between the objective situations of history and the subjective human response to that history, in order to draw forth what was for him a compelling and general human truth. Ōgai's favorite quotation from his much-loved Goethe suggests both his goal as a biographer of Chūsai and, by implication, the kind of methodology he was to create as he plunged deeper and deeper into the facts that he unearthed. "How may one come to know oneself? Never by contemplation, but only by action. Seek to do your duty, and you will know how it is with you. And what is your duty? The demands of the day." The examined life is thus closely related to the life in action.

Both Ōgai's treatment of Chūsai and Sartre's treatment of Flaubert have caused a certain amount of consternation to both writers and critics in their respective countries. Both writers have been accused of composing texts that lie outside the appropriate genres they appear to have appropriated for themselves. Sartre has been criticized for writing a disguised autobiography; Ōgai has been accused of "retreating into history." Even the presumably more flexible American disciplinary canons available to social scientists and literary scholars are perhaps too limited to find an adequate means to situate these two works. Readers open to the ambiguity and the fullness of human experience, however, have continued to admire and read both books, since the basic question they both pose, "What, at this point in time, can we know about a man?" transcends the sorts of closures usually considered appropriate to either social science or to literature. These mixtures of objective, historical, and subjective concerns suggest a special kind of authenticity capable of breaking open new areas of sensibility for their readers.

Both Sartre and Ōgai are, it seems to me, attempting to bring their own respective witness to bear on the fundamental problem of how reality is to be perceived. The "projects" of Flaubert and Chūsai, to borrow Sartre's term, require that their respective authors go beyond history, literature, or the social sciences as narrowly conceived. It is clear from the texts of both *The Family Idiot* and *Shibue Chūsai* that, while their authors believe in the irreducibility of historical facts, they nevertheless refuse to be limited by them. In writing on the genesis of another historical work, Ōgai, discussing his interjection of imagination into the data he had available to him, wrote concerning an incident he created: "At least I would like to think it happened that way. If I were writing a novel, I could merely write that it was so and not waste words in the fashion I have. . . . historians, seeing what I have written, will no doubt criticize me for my willfulness. Novelists, on the other hand, will laugh at my persistence."[11] Sartre for his part speaks of the fact that as "each piece of data is set in its place, [each] becomes a portion of the whole, which is constantly being created . . . a man is never an individual; it would be more fitting to call him a *universal singular.* Summed up and for this reason universalized by his epoch, he in turn resumes it by reproducing himself in it as singularity."[12]

In the end the work of both Sartre and of Ōgai reveals that the attitudes and the subjective motivations of the writer and the researcher are crucial and irreducible. A self-awareness of such compositional motives both on the part of the writer and his reader can thus allow for a particular richness of speculation which carries its own special freight of human truth. It takes courage to see significance beyond what are usually termed "objective facts," and many writers would prefer not to try. Sartre and Ōgai, each in his own way, realized the efficacy, indeed the inevitability, of the fact that wise and fruitful analysis begins with self-analysis. They had the courage to reveal themselves as well as what they knew of their putative subjects. Many critics of both writers have made the mistake of attempting to reduce this daring methodology to a matter of the subjectivity of the author and the quality of his individual personality. Yet Sartre and Ōgai did not merely slip into solipsism, into writing about themselves. Rather they seized the possibilities of a rich *reciprocity* between themselves, as authors, with their chosen material. Neither put themselves above their subjects, but had the peculiar courage to face the men they chose to portray on the most personal and intimate level. That reciprocity in turn allowed their examinations of motive, fact, and speculation to transcend the historical differences between them as writers and their subject matter. That reciprocity, finally, gives a profoundly human dimension to their studies, for the reader too can come to grasp, while learning the limitations of what he might ever "know," much that is important about Flaubert, Ōgai, Sartre, and Chūsai. Reflecting mirrors? Perhaps, but the images are sharp, and such reflections may represent the only level of historical truth that we can genuinely come to possess.

IV

THE JOURNEY INSIDE

8

The Theme of Pilgrimage
in Japanese Literature

JOHN UPDIKE, in reviewing a group of translations of Japanese fiction for the *New Yorker*, comments on Natsume Sōseki, perhaps the greatest of the novelists during the early part of the century, that Sōseki's "refusal to force his material toward pat conclusions or heightened climaxes represents a kind of negative power, that surrender to irregularity which is one of art's maneuvers of renewal."[1] In a sense his description might well turn out to serve as a compliment, although he may not have meant it that way. In a peculiar way Updike has caught a glimpse of one of the key strategies of traditional Japanese narrative technique. It is usually clear, even to a casual reader, that Japanese narrative depends much more on what might be termed lyric insight than on the clash of personality and the politics of power. All generalizations, of course, are dangerous; but it is probably safe to say that the thrust of Japanese prose writing is usually inward, with a narrative line pushing beyond plot, often beyond character, to a general realm of feeling with which the author hopes to put the reader in touch.

Here, by way of example, are crucial passages from two works acknowledged to be among the masterpieces of modern Japanese fiction. Both rely on traditional elements in narrative technique.

The first comes from the end of part 2 of Shiga Naoya's *Dark Night's Passing,* that long chronicle of personal salvation which occupied its author from 1921 until 1937. Shiga's protagonist, Kensaku, in search of peace and understanding, finds himself in a brothel. It is a moment in his life when he finds everything "stale and uninteresting."

When at last she came into the room, Kensaku was struck by how much less attractive she was than he had remembered her. True, when she smiled and showed her slightly crooked corner teeth she was strangely seductive; but in repose her face was distressingly ordinary. Feeling somewhat betrayed, he made no reference to the trip. She, too, kept silent about it, seemingly without conscious effort.

Yet when he reached out and held her round, heavy breast he was filled with an indefinable sense of comfort and satisfaction. It was as though he had touched something very precious. He let it rest on the palm of his hand, then shook it a little so that he could feel the full weight of it. There were no words to express the pleasure he experienced then. He continued to shake it gently, saying merely, "What riches!" It was for him somehow a symbol of all that was precious to him, of whatever it was that promised to fill the emptiness inside him.[2]

The passage is indeed a crucial one for the novel, yet it may hardly seem so to a Western reader, although in any case the moment can certainly be characterized as unforced. Shiga arranges that the reader should remain inside the flow of Kensaku's responses. The woman is no more than an object concerning which this meditation occurs. She (and most of the other characters in the novel) have no further function than to give rise to such states of mind, although those states themselves are remarkably varied. Then too the realm that the protagonist seeks throughout the novel is itself "beyond words"; in this particular scene, the object of meditation (a human breast) serves as a means to suggest a state to which Kensaku aspires, but which he cannot directly articulate, describe.

Here is a second passage, an important scene from Kawabata Yasunari's *Snow Country*, published in 1937. Shimamura, the protagonist, has been having an affair with a young geisha, Komako. Shimamura has decided toward the end of the novel that the relationship should be broken off.

He leaned against the brazier, provided against the coming of the snowy season, and thought how unlikely it was that he would come again once he had left. The innkeeper had lent him an old Kyoto tea-kettle, skillfully inlaid in silver with flowers and birds, and from it came the sound of wind in the pines. He could make out two pine breezes, as a matter of fact, a near one and a far one. Just beyond the far breeze he heard faintly the tinkling of a bell. He put his ear to the kettle and listened. Far away, where the bell tinkled on, he suddenly saw Komako's feet, tripping in time with the bell. He drew back. The time had come to leave.[3]

Here a decision to act is taken not through climactic action or confrontation, but by the juxtaposition of images that implant themselves on the sensibilities of the character. The power of these images, and the complexity of what they convey, force his decision, which might be characterized as a sort of deep psychic shift. Shimamura is in a state of receptivity such that he is able to reach a new level of sensitivity to the nuances of his own emotional situation.

Both Kawabata and Shiga knew and loved classical Japanese literature, and certainly the most representative of their works might well be described as a recasting, or metamorphosis, of some of the central concerns of traditional Japanese narrative, adapted so as to take into account certain psychological and artistic concerns central to both of these very twentieth-century authors.

One strategy common to both passages is the movement from a rational world of common-sense human reaction to a moment of high awareness, a sudden epiphany of heightened sensibility that occurs within the main character at the moment when some truth has been grasped or understood. This awareness may or may not produce movement within the subsequent narrative structure in terms of plot development or even character modification (just where one might expect that it could), but, by the same token, such moments do serve to justify and explain, at least in emotional terms, what has *preceded* the moment of truth that can sum up, and often break through, the conditions that led up to that sudden heightened consciousness. Indeed, the centrality of such moments in traditional Japanese literature has been of equal or greater importance in poetry and the *nō* drama than in the narrative. The traditional Japanese term used to describe this momentary state of awareness, in use as far back as the Heian period, is *aware,* that response by a person of sensibility to the world that can permit a sudden, intuitive understanding of the greatness, beauty, and often the sadness of life. *Aware,* perhaps the supreme traditional literary virtue that colors Lady Murasaki's eleventh-century *Tale of Genji,* has been amply described elsewhere and needs no extended discussion here.[4] What I would propose to focus on instead is the process by which those moments of informed enlightenment are achieved. For it is clear that in order to reach a state of *aware* some kind of displacement mechanism is required to lift and set aside the burdens and boundaries of common-sense thinking and feeling.

In seeking out an explanation of this process and of the methods by which it operates, it might seem that the simplest thing to do would be to turn to classical critical writings on Japanese prose in order to find an explication of the traditional Japanese view of the techniques involved. One discovers immediately, however, that no real systematic "poetics of prose" was attempted in Japan until the modern period, when a jumble of foreign assumptions about the nature and purposes of literature arrived to redefine the boundaries of artistic and literary concerns. This is not to say that no considerations of literature occurred in traditional writings; on the contrary, Zeami's writings on the aesthetics of the *nō* and in particular the various treatises on the composition of court poetry and, later, on *haiku* writing provide remarkable evidence of the skill and commitment felt by writers to seek the highest reaches of their craft. But in Japan, as in many other cultures, a set of hierarchies was developed early in the tradition. For cultivated Japanese from that time until the present century, "literature" in the best sense meant poetry, and prose writers who aspired to the conditions and possibilities of poetry came closest to achieving greatness. Once this assumption is understood, certain strategies of Japanese narrative, those seemingly "negative powers" that slightly perturbed John Updike, come into their own.

One of the earliest and most often quoted statements about the nature of Japanese poetry comes from the Japanese-language preface to the first great anthology of Japanese *waka* (thirty-one-syllable poems), the *Kokinshū* (Collection of Ancient and Modern Times), compiled about the year 905. In this preface its author, Ki no Tsurayuki (884–946), stresses the fact that poetry "has its seeds in man's heart . . . men's activities are various and whatever they say or hear touches their hearts and is expressed in poetry . . . poetry, without effort, can move heaven and earth, can touch the Gods and spirits."[5] In these seemingly simple words a relationship is struck at once between the poet and his or her primary material, an observation of nature itself. This relationship seems to involve as well the following assumptions: (1) poetry is based on human response; (2) that response must be natural, unforced, genuine; (3) poetry that results from such a response can in turn have the power to re-create that response in another. All of the relationships involved, however, must be genuine and spontaneous; nothing about them can be artificially constructed. These ideas certainly seem appropriate for a poetic form as short as a thirty-one-syllable *waka,* which remained the poetic standard for many centuries, and indeed such assumptions may seem too simple, perhaps merely obvious. Yet the dynamic they suggest is a powerful one that has shaped the whole development of Japanese aesthetics.

One might say then, in sum, that a poem at its best represents the creation in words of a moment of *aware,* the verbalization of a profound response to the deep truth reflected in a passing moment as felt by a person of genuine sensibility.

Such a hierarchy of response was as valued by the prose writers in this early period as by the poets. Indeed Ki no Tsurayuki himself, in one of the first great prose narratives in the classical Japanese canon, the *Tosa nikki (Tosa Diary)* of 936, states, or has his putative authoress state, that the artistic impulse must arise from the irrepressible feelings of the observer, feelings that cannot remain unrecorded. Aboard a ship, the narrator looks at the passing scenery on the coastline and records a poem written by one of the passengers, adding the remark that "it is impossible merely to look upon the splendor of this scenery."[6] Later, remembering her dead child, she writes a poem, then comments that "I do not set down these words nor did I compose the poem, out of mere love of writing. Surely both in China and in Japan art is that which is created when we are unable to suppress our feelings."[7]

This attitude prefigures the famous section in the "Fireflies" chapter of *The Tale of Genji,* when Genji discusses the purposes of fiction with Tamakazura, the daughter of his best friend, To no Chūjō. Genji there states his belief that, despite a certain level of fabrication inherent in fiction, "real emotion" and "a plausible chain of events" can often be found.

> He smiled. "What would we do if there were not these old romances to relieve our boredom? But amid all the fabrication I must admit that I do find real emotions and plausible chains of events. We can be quite aware of the frivolity and the idleness and still be moved. We have to feel a little sorry for a charming princess in the depths of gloom. Some-

times a series of absurd and grotesque incidents which we know to be quite improbable holds our interest, and afterwards we must blush that it was so. Yet even then we can see what it was that held us. Sometimes I stand and listen to the stories they read to my daughter, and I think to myself that there certainly are good talkers in the world. I think that these yarns must come from people much practiced in lying. But perhaps that is not the whole of the story?"

She pushed away her inkstone. "I can see that that would be the view of someone much given to lying himself. For my part, I am convinced of their truthfulness."

He laughed. "I have been rude and unfair to your romances, haven't I. They have set down and preserved happenings from the age of the gods to our own. *The Chronicles of Japan* and the rest are a mere fragment of the whole truth. It is your romances that fill in the details.

"We are not told of things that happened to specific people exactly as they happened; but the beginning is when there are good things and bad things, things that happen in this life which one never tires of seeing and hearing about, things which one cannot bear not to tell of and must pass on for all generations. If the storyteller wishes to speak well, then he chooses the good things; and if he wishes to hold the reader's attention he chooses bad things, extraordinarily bad things. Good things and bad things alike, they are things of this world and no other."[8]

Genji's statements indicate an artistic commitment to a close and reciprocal relationship between the author and his or her observed material. Crucial to an appropriate response is the author's own sensibility, so that with a requisite understanding his or her reactions can be written down in an artistic form that will have the power to evoke similar responses in others. Without that sensibility the writer will not be able to undergo the kind of displacement necessary to achieve such a higher awareness. In this reciprocal relationship, then, a high level of cultivation and sensitivity of the author is central.

As poetic theory developed in Japan, the writing of poetry itself continued and developed among the courtier class as a social craft, albeit of the highest standards. As time passed, however, the question inevitably arose as to how an aspiring poet might educate himself or herself in order to become an adept in the art of poetry. One particularly elegant and informative document that deals with this subject is an informal treatise on poetry entitled the *Mumyōshō* (Miscellaneous Notes) composed by the writer Kamo no Chōmei some time after

1200, roughly three hundred years after Ki no Tsurayuki's celebrated *Kokinshū* preface quoted above. Throughout, Chōmei indicates that while the art of poetry can be learned to a certain extent through a study and assimilation of past masters, such knowledge and discipline must be allied to a kind of natural ease, perhaps something like that which an athlete gains after years of rigorous training. Those who are unwilling or unable to subject themselves to finding this ease beyond rigor will never compose naturally.

> When you have a scene of simple beauty you should let your words follow the flow of the common language, for when you try too much to think out something, you get, on the contrary, expressions that sound conspicuous. This is like twining a thread; when trying to twine it neatly, you overdo the job, you get a knot. Someone who can size this up well is skillful. Atmosphere is something that develops of itself, and yet it is necessary to make an effort to achieve it according to the occasion; if you are skillful in this you will be able to see the distinction. Thus, in the brilliant phrases of bad poets many shortcomings are bound to arise.[9]

Effort alone will not suffice; poetry cannot be willed but must well up as a spontaneous response, later to be captured in writing. Chōmei provides a wry example of too much study gone wrong.

> I have heard that when Lord Toshinari's daughter composes for court recitation, she goes through different anthologies a few days before the event, reading them with care again and again, and when she feels that she has read enough, she puts everything aside, dims her lamp and, shutting herself off from other people, puts her mind to work. The Kunaikyō keeps books and scrolls open around her from beginning to end, uses a shortened lamp stand to have the light close and works at her poems day and night without break. This lady has become sick because of excessive concentration on the composition of poetry and has once been on the verge of death. Her father, a Zen Priest, warned her: 'Everything depends on your being alive. How can you be so absorbed in your poetry that you become sick!' But she did not listen to his advice, and when she finally died it must have been because of an accumulation of such things.[10]

For Chōmei it is the suggestion of the ineffable, grasped by the poet's intuition, that gives greatness to the art of poetry. In writing on the literary quality of *yūgen*, the so-called style of "mystery and depth" that was to become the great artistic virtue of medieval Japan, Chōmei, again echoing Tsurayuki, shares his conviction that the truth lies, must lie, behind the immediately visible.

> Only when many ideas are compressed in one word, when without displaying it you exhaust your mind in all its depth and you imagine the imperceptible, when commonplace things are used to display beauty and in a style of naiveté an idea is developed to the limit, only then, when thinking does not lead anywhere and words are inadequate, should you express your feelings by this method which has the capacity to move heaven and earth and the power to touch the gods and spirits.[11]

In the art of poetry, and so by extension in the art of prose as well, the author's sensibilities and skills must be such that these ineffable responses to the world can find proper means of recording in words. Chōmei talks a great deal in his treatise about how to arrange those words into *waka*, but he never discusses how the poet, so central to this process, can achieve the necessary personal displacement from the ordinary world. Chōmei merely indicates that the poet must first have the experience, or at the least an intimation or imagination of it, before any suitable poem can be written. For it is the actual experience, on whatever level, that provides the ultimate authenticity of any work of art.

The *haiku* poet Matsuo Bashō (1644–1694), writing four centuries later, did attempt, in a highly figurative way, to suggest to one of his students what the displacement process actually might involve. These passages were cited earlier, but they are worth quoting again in the present context.

> What is important is to keep our mind high in the world of true understanding, and returning to the world of our daily experience to seek therein the truth of beauty. No matter what we may be doing at a given moment, we must not forget that it has a bearing on our everlasting self which is poetry.[12]

Then again:

Go to the pine if you want to learn about the pine, or to the bamboo if you want to learn about the bamboo. And in doing so, you must leave your subjective preoccupation with yourself. Otherwise you impose yourself on the object and do not learn. Your poetry issues of its own accord when you and the object have become one—when you have plunged deep enough into the object to see something like a hidden glimmering there. However well phrased your poetry may be, if your feeling is not natural—if the object and yourself are separate—then your poetry is not true poetry but merely your subjective counterfeit.[13]

What Bashō hints at here is precisely this kind of displacement from commonplace concerns that seems fundamental to the tradition; both the artist and the event witnessed must move each other out of the ordinary into a "world of true understanding." Art then becomes the means by which this experience can be conveyed to others.[14]

In searching for a means to attempt to sketch out a systematic understanding of this process and to discover the nature of that displacement at which Bashō hinted, I have been aided, as I have mentioned in earlier chapters, by the insights I have gained from the work of the anthropologist Victor Turner and his writings on the process of pilgrimage. Turner set out to study the process of pilgrimage in actual life, not in literature, and his copious and telling examples are drawn from historically documented or contemporary sources. Japan does not figure among them. Yet by the model he develops, and by his description of the psychological relationships he believes are involved on the part of the pilgrims who join in the process, his analysis can provide a definition of the process of pilgrimage that resembles in a striking fashion the experiences of displacement suggested by Bashō in the text cited above. Turner's model thus helps to explain the process of lyric movement found in both Japanese poetry and prose. It is my contention that the sorts of "units" or "kernels" that, strung together, make up the flow of Japanese narrative (such as the two extracts from the novels I cited at the beginning of this chapter) represent a kind of literary construction of this pilgrimage process, a working out into words of the mechanism Turner explicates.

If the pilgrim follows certain procedures, Turner indicates, he can enter into that state of communal, intuitive understanding. Then, when he returns to the real world, he can gain from that experience a new understanding that, once grasped, can remain with him in his ordinary life.

How to cross over that threshold? From his anthropological research, Turner posits several conditions. First of all, the pilgrim must wish to undergo the experience. Secondly, the pilgrim must move out of his ordinary, known environment and travel to an unknown, holy place. Such places are usually away from urban centers, where the atmosphere will be more conducive to the development of a heightened awareness. Then too the pilgrim must abandon his ordinary sense of time. For a pilgrim who crosses over into a state of enlightenment, space will seem altered, and time will seem to change its dimensions. Turner has supplied a number of striking examples of statements made by pilgrims from a wide variety of cultures, both historical and contemporary, which corroborate his insights.

Seen in this fashion, Bashō's remarks quoted above can also serve as such a witness and illustrate how well this secular pilgrim's testimony fits Turner's model. Go to nature; forget yourself; forget time; return to the world to share what you know with others.

Turner's model is a rich and suggestive one and its potential applications are many. I would like here to make a comparison between Turner's pilgrim, who moves across a "threshold" to a greater awareness, and the prose writer who moves a created protagonist, or on occasion the protagonist's mind, from an ordinary comprehension of reality to a moment of insight, an epiphany of *aware*. Often this displacement is accomplished, in terms of language, by changing from prose to poetry, or, in some cases, as close to poetry as the appropriate style of composition may allow. There are endless examples in both traditional and modern Japanese literature of such literary displacements. I would like to point out three varieties here.

The first of them involves a description of the physical movements of the character involved. In examples found in traditional Japanese narrative, such a character might well have been a Buddhist pilgrim. And the same sort of process carries on in modern life. Kensaku, the protagonist of Shiga's *Dark Night's Passing,* finishes his travail, and perhaps his life, on a pilgrimage to Mount Daisen on the west coast of Japan. These scenes make up the final chapters of the novel. Shimamura's trips to the snow country too might be regarded as a series of pilgrimages away from ordinary life, an attempt to seek out the meaning of nature, his own nature, and the relationship between the two.

All of such secular pilgrimages are reinforced by the presence in the literary tradition of such potent historical and cultural figures as Saigyō (1118–1190), who withdrew from the Heian court to become a travelling monk and who left behind him, in his *waka,* a record of his spiritual searchings. Saigyō's travels and his encounters became the stuff of legends that produced later fanciful accounts of him in the *nō* theatre, genre painting, and produced as well many homages to his example in later poetry and prose. Travelling, whether sacred or secular, served as a form of displacement and gave rise to a special type of literary narrative, the *michiyuki,* or "account of a journey." Such accounts are perhaps most familiar because of their inclusion as scenes in such theatrical works as the medieval *nō* dramas and the puppet plays by Chikamatsu and others in the later Tokugawa period (1600–1868), but this form of travel account can be traced all the way back to scenes of travel in the *Man'yōshū,* the earliest collection of Japanese poetry, compiled in the eighth century.

By the medieval period this literary genre of a physical displacement leading to moments of personal insight had become a recognized feature of prose narrative. By way of example, book 10, chapter 6 of *The Tale of the Heike,* the great work that chronicles the 1185 civil wars that destroyed the power of the court, contains just such an account. In this section, Shigehira, one of the Taira generals, is captured and sent to Kamakura, the capital of his enemies, the Minamoto. As Shigehira makes the trip he is put in contact with places that have historical and poetic associations familiar to him. These encounters thus give rise in him to a sense of the fleetingness of his own life.

> When he came to the banks of the Shinomiya River, he remembered a thatched hut belonging to Semimaru, the fourth son of Emperor Daigo, near the Osaka Checkpoint. It had been there that Semimaru had calmed his mind in the mountain breeze to play the biwa. Lord Hiromasa of the third court rank went to listen to his biwa at this spot day after day, night after night, for three long years. He made these trips on windy days or calm, on rainy nights or fine. Thus pacing up

and down, or standing near the hut, he strained his ears and mastered the three secret melodies. Now a sense of profound pathos welled up in Shigehira as he passed this area.[15]

Sights of natural beauty mix with literary recollection. In order to manifest this heightened sense of beauty, the language of the text takes on a poetic rhythm mixing allusion with verbal cadence in a fashion that no translation can encompass. The trip also permits Shigehira a mysterious encounter with the legendary Yuya, a consort of Lord Munemori and the subject of an important *nō* play. Such a fanciful meeting, without any basis in historical fact, could only take place in the kind of poetic environment provided by the occasion of the pilgrimage.

Later, Shigehira passes a spot where the monk Saigyō wrote a poem, and, by empathy with the poet's art, comes to feel in himself the same sense of *aware* that allowed Saigyō to compose his poem.

> When he came to Saya-no-Nakayama, his heart sank, for he remembered the melancholy poem that had been composed by the priest Saigyō at this very spot:
>
> > After I have grown
> > Bent under the weight of years
> > I am here again
> > —Saya-no-Nakayama—
> > I have lived beyond my span.[16]

Eventually, he sees Mount Fuji.

> Passing by the Kiyomi Checkpoint, he entered the plain at the foot of Mount Fuji. To the north the pine trees rustled in the wind. Beyond them lay the green slope of the mountain. To the south, the waves lapped at the beach. Vast was the blue ocean.[17]

When Shigehira arrives in Kamakura, the poetic interlude is over, and the displacement (and the chapter) are finished; in the next section, prose and politics take over again, as Shigehira comes to know his own cruel fate. Yet the *michiyuki* travelling scene has performed a function in the narrative that goes beyond that of a simple colorful interlude. Both the emotions of the character and the language in which the character and his surroundings are described have moved into a realm of heightened sensitivity that in this case permit the protagonist, through the sense of the pathos of human life that he has gained, to face his own fate with greater nobility and self-understanding. His trip into himself has paralleled his trip along the road.

The pilgrimage process can be observed as well in Japanese narrative when no physical displacement whatsoever is involved. I would like to cite here two examples of another kind of displacement that leads the protagonist to a heightened awareness, a process that might be termed *psychological* displacement.

One type of such displacement involves the function of memory. The use of memories of the past, particularly of past felicities, serves as a common device throughout classical Japanese literature. A pilgrimage into the past of the character, as he or she traces threads of personal and emotional history, produces an epiphany, an intuitive grasp of profound personal realities. Here, for example, is an example, chosen almost at random from an important work of the Heian period, the *Sarashina nikki,* or *Sarashina Diary,* translated by Ivan Morris and given the English title *As I Crossed a Bridge of Dreams.* The process of emotional displacement is obvious.

> We now had to move into a new house. The old one had been a spacious place that gave one the feeling of being deep in the mountains; and our garden with its Spring blossoms and Autumn leaves had far outshone the surrounding hills. The present house, which had a tiny garden and no trees at all, was smaller than anything I had seen, and the move saddened me greatly. The garden opposite was full of plum trees, which blossomed in a profusion of red and white; when there was a breeze, their scent wafted towards me. One day, overcome with memories of the old house to which I had grown so accustomed, I composed the poem,
>
> > *From the neighbouring garden comes a scented breeze.*
> > *Deeply I breathe it in, though longing all the while*
> > *For the plum tree by our ancient eaves.* [18]

This prose paragraph and the following poem constitute one reciprocal unit. The paragraph begins with a simple statement, "We now had to move into a new house." The succeeding phrases go on to add memories of the old house, a comparison is made between the two, and the narrator's resulting sense of loss leads to her attempt to capture in a poem the truth of the emotional reality of that loss. The idea of loss then links the reader to the next section, which concerns a deeper human loss, the death of the narrator's elder sister. Such linkages propel the narrative forward, providing a consistence of emotional momentum that functions in much the same way as plot can function in Western narrative. This sort of emotional unit is as central to the structure of Kawabata's *Snow Country* as it is to Lady Murasaki's *Tale of Genji*.

Memory can serve as one means of displacement leading to self-understanding; desire can serve as another. Ihara Saikaku (1642–1693), the Tokugawa *haiku* poet and novelist whose satiric accounts of the foibles of his society continue to charm readers in and out of Japan, makes a full and quite self-conscious use of what were to him traditionally serious literary devices. Here, by way of contrast, is a comic *michiyuki* scene from book 3 of *Five Women Who Loved Love* (1686). The two lovers, Mōemon and Osan, flee their responsibilities and disappear into the wilderness. Saikaku plays on the expectations of his readers, who are gradually led to feel the despair of the pair.

> Hand in hand, Mōemon and Osan trekked across the wilderness of Tamba. They had to make their own road through the stubborn underbrush. At last they climbed a high peak, and looking back whence they had come, reflected on the terrors of their journey. It was, to be sure, the lot they had chosen; still, there was little pleasure in living on in the role of the dead. They were lost souls, miserably lost, on a route that was not even marked by a woodsman's footprints. Osan stumbled feebly along, so wretched that she seemed to be gasping for what might be her last breath, and her face lost all its color. Mōemon tried every means to revive and sustain his beloved, even catching spring water in a leaf as it dripped from the rocks. But Osan had little strength left to draw on. Her pulse beat more and more faintly; any minute might be her last.[19]

Then, by a sudden twist, he reminds the reader of the pair's true nature.

> Mōemon could offer nothing at all in the way of medicine. He stood by helplessly to wait for Osan's end, then suddenly bent near and whispered in her ear, "Just a little farther on we shall come to the village of some people I know. There we can forget all our misery, indulge our hearts' desire with pillows side by side, and talk again of love!"

When she heard this, Osan felt better right away. "How good that sounds! Oh, you are worth paying with one's life for!"[20]

Put in touch with their real selves, the two now continue on in search of an appropriate spot for their desired tryst. The theme of this "unit," desire, is linked as well to the next incident, in which Osan finds herself caught with a marriage proposal from a bumptious country hunter, a proposal that has been brought about by the desire of Mōemon's aunt, not for physical pleasure but for money. Again the links from unit to unit in the narrative structure are constructed by a procession of connected emotional states and attitudes, not through any plot devices. The "truth" of the narrative, whether in the humorous stance of Saikaku or in the lyric mode of the author of the *Sarashina Diary* lies in the believability of the manifested emotional state. In terms of the Japanese tradition, an effective narrative structure will function so as to cast these states before the reader in a convincing way.

Still a third kind of displacement might be termed a literary displacement, in which the protagonist is moved toward an intuitive grasp of reality not through any direct personal or emotional displacement but rather through an encounter with a literary statement that can conjure up a sense of essential meaning so powerful that an appropriate range of response wells up naturally in the protagonist. This kind of displacement can be found in the earliest of the prose narratives. In the *Tosa Diary*, for example, the narrator, stranded in a harbor as her ship awaits better weather, remembers the voyage of Abe no Nakamaro, an envoy dispatched to China in 717, where, after an unsuccessful attempt to make the difficult trip back to Japan, he remained for the rest of his life.

> I am having great difficulty sleeping. The moon is in its twentieth night. There are no hills or mountains whose rim it might rise above, as it does in the capital, so it just seems to come out of the sea. It must have been just this kind of moon from the sea that, ages ago, was seen by Abe no Nakamaro from the coast of China. When he was returning to this country, at the place where he was to board the ship the men of that country gave him a farewell banquet and, in regret of his departure, composed proper Chinese poems and performed other things for him. Perhaps because they had not been able to express their reluctance to part adequately, he stayed with them till the twentieth night of

the moon. His moon, too, must have risen from the sea. It was on looking at it that Lord Nakamaro said, "In our country we have composed
poems since the age of the gods. The gods themselves have done so,
and now people of whatever rank make poems of this kind to show their
regret at parting and to express their joys or their sorrows." Telling
them of this, he composed the following poem.

> I cast my eyes
> Wide across the blue plains of the sea
> Brilliant with a moon—
> Can it be the one that in far Kasuga
> Rises over the hilltop of Mikasa?[21]

Remembering Abe's poem, the narrator reflects on the fact that
the emotional responses of human beings to nature transcend any
cultural differences, and this thought in turn creates in the narrator
an emotional response that then triggers her own poem.

> China and this country have different languages, but since the radi-
> ance of the moon is the same for both, men's feelings about it must
> surely be the same. The recollections of that distant age led to a poem.
>
> > This is the very moon
> > That we see upon the mountain's rim
> > In the capital,
> > But here the moon arises from the waves
> > And back into the waves it sets.[22]

The initial displacement in this example is literary, but the results
are the same; what has been produced is an outpouring of an emotional response, genuine and unforced, to a truth "about which men
cannot remain silent."

My catalogue of displacements, or movements, is by no means
complete, but I hope that I have at least been able to suggest how this
powerful literary and psychological device can operate under a variety of circumstances, each arranged so as to permit a strategy for
propelling the reader toward the truth of an emotional state the
writer wishes to intimate. In this regard it might be useful to indicate
briefly the function of language in bringing about this epiphany of
feeling. Much of what I can mention will already seem obvious from
a reading of the examples above, yet some indication of the techniques employed will reinforce the ideas of pilgrimage that I have
attempted to describe. Linguistically speaking, then, the reader is led

from the ordinary, descriptive world of prose across a mysterious line into that realm of cultivated, natural response represented, from the beginnings of the tradition, by the province of poetry. And, as I suggested above, any one series of movements from prose to poetry, taken together, can often be considered as one narrative unit.

The basic ordering of these units in terms of language usually involves a sequence of three subunits: ordinary prose; a more lyric, introspective prose; and a final poem. The possible variations are many, but the general growth of momentum from slow to fast is basic to them all.[23] Here, for example, is an example from chapter 20, "Morning Glory," of Lady Murasaki's *Tale of Genji*. In this section Genji comes to visit his friend the Fifth Princess on a winter day. He arrives in a rather glum state after witnessing the displeasure of his chief consort, Murasaki, at his departure.

> He sent one of his men in through the great west gate. The Fifth Princess, who had not expected him so late on a snowy evening, made haste to order the gate opened. A chilly-looking porter rushed out. He was having trouble and there was no one to help him.
> "All rusty," he muttered. Genji felt rather sorry for him.
> And so thirty years had gone by, like yesterday and today. It was a fleeting, insubstantial world, and yet the temporary lodgings which it offered were not easy to give up. The grasses and flowers of the passing seasons continued to pull at him.
> > "And when did wormwood overwhelm this gate,
> > This hedge, now under snow, so go to ruin?"
> Finally the gate was opened and he made his way in.[24]

The sound of the rusty locks throws Genji into a reverie over the ineffability of his own life; yet as he realizes that he can still respond to the power of nature, the unit ends with a poem that combines both ideas in a joint image of the futility of human endeavor and a season appropriate to that emotion.

All the linguistic parts of the unit fit together so as to reinforce each other. The prose explains the poem, and the poem recapitulates and dignifies the prose. Neither prose nor poetry could attain the desired level of significance without the other. Together, they work beautifully. In modern fiction, of course, poetry is not usually possible. These epiphanies tend to occur as striking images, in short prose poems.

In fact, the classical poetic tradition has always had a need for prose. The kind of lyric outburst possible in a thirty-one-syllable *waka* often deserves a context, a setting, or some sort of explanation so that its message can be adequately conveyed. In this regard, the role of description and clarification assigned to prose in traditional narrative style is crucial.

One revealing example of a felt need for the reciprocity of poetry and prose can be found in one of the classic texts of the tenth century, *The Tales of Ise,* a mixture of more than two hundred poems, many by one of the greatest of the early Japanese poets, Ariwara no Narihira (825–880). A close examination of the text, however, shows that many of the prose sections were later added to the poems, a great number of which appear without such prose contexts in various imperial poetry anthologies. The following will illustrate something of how the amalgam worked.

The poem quoted below, attributed to Narihira, appears in the *Gosenshū* (Later Collection), the second imperial anthology compiled about 950, roughly the time of the compilation of *The Tales of Ise.* The poem, of course, was written something like a hundred years before. In the poetry anthology the poem is included in the "Autumn" section and conjures up an image of the changing seasons.

> Dancing fireflies,
> If you can soar
> Above the clouds,
> Tell the wild goose
> Of the autumnal breeze.[25]

In *The Tales of Ise,* however, the poem is given a lengthy prose preface which creates a story that might plausibly give rise to the emotions expressed in the poem. In order to do so, the compilers evidently did not hesitate to change the season so as to intensify the mood. Read alone, the poem seems to suggest little of the meaning drawn out of it, or imposed upon it, by the prose statement that was later added.

> Once there was a carefully reared girl who longed desperately to tell a certain man of her love for him. At length she fell ill—broken hearted, perhaps, because she could devise no way of letting him know—and as she lay dying she confessed her attachment. When her father learned of it he sent word to the man, weeping bitterly.

The man hurried to the house, only to find the girl dead. Feeling strangely bereaved, he stayed to mourn for her. It was late in the Sixth Month and exceedingly hot. Music was performed in the evening to comfort the departed spirit, and as the night deepened a cool breeze began to stir. Fireflies danced high in the air. Staring out at the insects from where he lay, the man recited,

> Dancing fireflies,
> If you can soar
> Above the clouds,
> Tell the wild goose
> Of the autumnal breeze.[26]

Modern commentators posit that the flying geese represent a metaphor for the soul of the dead girl, and that the fireflies thus carry a message to her spirit, but little of this level of meaning seems suggested in the original. Whatever the intentions of the original poet, the compilers of *The Tales of Ise* sought to deepen and expand the world of the poem by creating a reciprocity between the original poem and the preface they composed.

No writer in the Japanese tradition understood these reciprocal relationships better than Matsuo Bashō, who in his travel diaries brought this kind of first-person interior narrative to its greatest heights. One of the most famous passages in his 1694 *Narrow Road to the Deep North* provides a truly splendid example of the displacement process and can well serve as a model of Japanese narrative strategy at its most polished. Every element is successfully combined. The narrator, himself the literary persona Bashō, is on a secular, poetic pilgrimage to see the places where the great poets of the past found inspiration. He arrives at Hiraizumi, the furthest point north to which he will travel on the east coast of Japan, to visit the ruins of the court established there by Fujiwara Kiyohira in 1094. After a decisive victory in the 1185 civil wars, Minamoto Yoritomo decided to do away with his possible rival, his enormously popular younger brother Yoshitsune. Yoshitsune fled from Yoritomo as far north as Hiraizumi, at which point he, and the city, were destroyed. The incident is one of the most famous in Japanese history, and so it is not surprising that Bashō, almost five hundred years later, should know every detail of those happenings. Here is the section from the diary concerning Bashō's visit.

The splendors of the three generations of Hiraizumi now comprise the briefest of dreams, and of the grand facade there are only faint

remains stretching out for two and a half miles. Hidehira's castle is now
leveled to overgrown fields, and of all the splendors of his past, only
Mount Kinkei retains its form. Climbing up to the high ramparts of
what had been Yoshitsune's stronghold, one can see below the Kitakami River flowing in a wide stream from the south. The Koromo
River pours past the site of loyal Izumi Saburō's castle, then beneath
these ramparts, and at last into the Kitakami. The old relics of others
like Yasuhira are to be found separated to the west at Koromo Barrier,
which controlled the southern approach and probably was meant to
protect the area against incursions by the northern tribesmen. Yoshitsune and his brave adherents took refuge in this citadel, but the most
famous names claim the world only a little while, and now the level
grass covers their traces. What Tu Fu wrote came to my mind—
     The country crumbles, but mountains and rivers endure;
     A late spring visits the castle, replacing it with green grasses . . .
and sitting down on my pilgrim's hat I wept over the ruins of time.
          The summer grasses:
     The high bravery of men-at-arms,
          The vestiges of dream.[27]

The construction of the prose passage begins with description and
observation. We are told what the poet actually saw. Then the narrator moves to memory, a memory of Yoshitsune and his tragic end.
The succeeding movement is from the specific (Yoshitsune) to the
general (the meaninglessness of fame). This movement in turn
sparks a literary reference that provides resonance to the poet's own
thoughts about the meaning of time. Bashō quotes two lines of the
great T'ang-dynasty poet Tu Fu (712–770), which are among the most
famous in Chinese poetry. Their evocative power and the poet's own
natural flow of feeling cause him to weep "over the ruins of time."
Then, in a final burst of emotion "which one cannot bear not to tell
of and must pass on for all generations," Bashō concludes with his
own *haiku* on the insignificance of humanity before the immensity of
time.
     The inward thrust of Japanese narrative prose does not then center
on the kind of "heightened climax" that John Updike missed in his
reading of Sōseki. Rather, in the Japanese tradition the climax of any
sequence lies not in the event itself but rather in the genuineness and
spontaneity of the human response to that event. Interestingly
enough, it is the existence of that inward quality in even the oldest
texts in the Japanese tradition that makes so many of the great Japa-

nese works, classic and modern alike, surprisingly accessible to the modern Western reader. For whatever our differences, the narrator of the *Tosa Diary* might surely have included us as well in her thoughts when she wrote that "China and this country have different languages, but since the radiance of the moon is the same for both, men's feelings about it must surely be the same." The strategies of so many of the great narrative works in the Japanese tradition lie in an ability to ease us into that realm of feelings. Politics? Confrontation? The clash of ideas? These can all be found in certain modern Japanese works, but these represent comparatively recent developments, and must, as Lady Murasaki might have said at the end of one of her chapters, detain us on another day.

Notes

CHAPTER I: *Aware* on the Seine

1. Edward Seidensticker, *Kafū the Scribbler* (Stanford: Stanford University Press, 1965).
2. Matsuo Bashō, *The Narrow Road to the Deep North and Other Travel Sketches*, trans. Nobuyuki Yuasa (Baltimore: Penguin Classics, 1966), p. 28.
3. Ibid., p. 33.
4. Ibid., p. 71.
5. Ibid., p. 97.
6. *Tōson zenshū*, (Tokyo: Chikuma shobō, 1967), vol. 6, *Paris dayori* (News from Paris), p. 246.
7. Ibid.
8. Ibid., p. 299.
9. Ibid., p. 309.
10. Ibid., p. 399.
11. Ibid., p. 304.
12. *Tōson zenshū*, vol. 8, *Étranger* (Stranger), p. 287.
13. Ibid., p. 363.
14. Ibid., p. 429.
15. Shimazaki Tōson, *Shinsei* (A New Life), 2 vols. (Tokyo: Iwanami shoten, 1966–1967).
16. Ibid., vol. 1, p. 129.
17. Ibid., vol. 1, pp. 205–206.
18. Ibid., vol. 1, p. 186.
19. Ibid., vol. 1, p. 256.
20. Ibid., vol. 2, p. 139.
21. *Paris dayori*, p. 441.
22. Ibid., p. 448.
23. *Étranger*, p. 441.

24. The basic explication of Turner's concepts can be found in his *Dramas, Fields, and Metaphors: Symbolic Action in Human Society* (Ithaca: Cornell University Press, 1974). For a helpful explanation of these ideas with particular reference to Japan, see William LaFleur, "Points of Departure: Comments on Religious Pilgrimage in Sri Lanka and Japan," *Journal of Asian Studies* 38, no. 2 (February 1979): 271–281.

25. *Shinsei,* vol. 1, p. 121.

CHAPTER 2: Three Japanese Painters in Paris

1. For the full poem in translation, see Hiroaki Sato and Burton Watson, *From the Country of Eight Islands* (New York: Anchor/Doubleday, 1981), pp. 464–467.

2. Cited in Chisaburoh F. Yamada, ed., *Dialogue in Art, Japan and the West* (Tokyo and New York: Kodansha International, 1976), p. 103.

CHAPTER 3: Kishida Kunio

1. *Kishida Kunio zenshū* (Tokyo: Shinchōsha, 1955), vol. 9, pp. 61–62.

2. A. G. Lehmann, "The Writer as Canary," in *Literature and Politics in the Twentieth Century,* ed. Walter Laqueur and George L. Mosse (New York: Harper and Row, 1967), p. 19.

3. *Kishida Kunio zenshū,* vol. 1, p. 88.

4. Ibid., vol. 2, pp. 412–413.

5. Ibid., vol. 10, p. 19.

6. The Japanese text for the play translated here can be found in *Kishida Kunio zenshū,* vol. 1, pp. 77–86.

CHAPTER 4: Mokuami's Evil One and Her Modern Counterpart

1. For some extended remarks on Yashiro and a full English version of another of his plays, *Hokusai Sketchbooks,* see Ted T. Takaya, ed. and trans., *Modern Japanese Drama, an Anthology* (New York: Columbia University Press, 1979).

2. Yashiro Seiichi, *Dokufu no chichi* (Tokyo: Kawade shobo, 1979), p. 222.

3. Ibid., pp. 96–97.

4. Ibid., p. 94.

5. Kawatake Mokuami, *Toji-awase Oden no kanabumi* (Tokyo: Shunyodo, 1926), vol. 24, p. 819.

6. Ibid., p. 825.
7. Ibid., p. 846.
8. Ibid., p. 850.
9. Georg Lukàcs, *The Historical Novel* (Harmondsworth: Penguin Books, 1969), pp. 150–151.
10. Ibid., p. 156.
11. Jean Duvignaud, "The Theatre in Society: Society in Theatre," in *Sociology of Literature and Drama,* ed. Elizabeth and Tom Burns (Harmondsworth: Penguin Books, 1973), p. 90.
12. *Hamlet,* act 5, lines 393–400.

CHAPTER 5: Japanese Theatre

1. Peter Arnott, *The Theatres of Japan* (New York: St. Martin's Press, 1969), p. 228.
2. Paul Claudel, *L'Échange* (Paris: Mercure de France, 1964), pp. 32–34. My translation.
3. For a full translation, see Thomas Rimer, "Zeami," *Monumenta Nipponica* 25, nos. 3–4 (1970): 431–435.
4. Ibid., p. 434.
5. Ibid., p. 435.
6. Ibid.
7. Ibid., p. 437.
8. Ibid., p. 440.
9. Ibid., p. 443.
10. Ibid., p. 444.
11. Ibid., p. 445.
12. Ibid.
13. Arnold Hauser, *The Social History of Art* (New York: Vintage Books, 1951), vol. 3, p. 90.
14. Donald Keene, trans., *Major Plays of Chikamatsu* (New York: Columbia University Press, 1961), pp. 419–420.
15. Ibid., p. 421.
16. Ibid., p. 420.
17. Ibid., p. 422.
18. Ibid., p. 423.
19. Ibid., p. 424.
20. Ibid., p. 425.
21. Georg Lukàcs, "The Sociology of Modern Drama," in *The Theory of the Modern Stage,* ed. Eric Bentley (Harmondsworth: Penguin Books, 1968), p. 429.

22. Ibid., p. 438.

23. Yamazaki Masakazu, *Mask and Sword: Two Plays for the Modern Japanese Theatre* (New York: Columbia University Press, 1980), pp. 127–128.

24. Ibid., pp. 167–168.

25. Ibid., p. 169.

26. Ibid., p. 181.

CHAPTER 6: The Pilgrimage of Personality

1. Philip Rieff, *The Triumph of the Therapeutic* (New York: Harper and Row, 1956), p. 2.

2. Ibid., p. 31.

3. "Kamo no Chōmei," in *Yōkyoku shosho,* ed. Haga Yasuichi and Sasaki Nobutsuna (Tokyo: Hakubunkan, 1914), vol. 1, p. 506.

4. Kamo no Chōmei, *An Account of My Hut,* in Donald Keene, *Anthology of Japanese Literature* (New York: Grove Press, 1955), p. 208.

5. Ibid.

6. John H. Rosenfield, "The Unity of the Three Creeds: A Theme in Japanese Ink Painting of the Fifteenth Century," in *Japan in the Muromachi Age,* ed. J. W. Hall and T. Takeshi (Berkeley: University of California Press, 1977), pp. 211–214.

7. J. T. Rimer, "An Interview with Yamazaki Masakazu," *Denver Quarterly* 12, no. 2 (Summer 1977): 176.

8. *Yōkyoku shosho,* vol. 1, p. 511.

9. Kamo, *An Account of My Hut,* p. 211.

10. Nishiwaki Junzaburō, "A Pastoral," in *Nishiwaki Junzaburō zenshū* (Tokyo: Chikuma Shobō, 1973), vol. 9, p. 746.

11. Ibid., pp. 747–748.

CHAPTER 7: Mori Ōgai and Jean-Paul Sartre

1. Jean-Paul Sartre, *The Family Idiot,* trans. Carol Cosman (Chicago: University of Chicago Press, 1981), p. ix.

2. See, for example, various entries in Michael Ermarth, *Wilhelm Dilthey: The Critique of Historical Reason* (Chicago: University of Chicago Press, 1978), for an explanation of this complex term.

3. In the case of Sartre the reader is particularly fortunate to have a wise guide to this difficult text in *Sartre & Flaubert* by Hazel Barnes (Chicago: University of Chicago Press, 1981).

4. Sartre, *The Family Idiot,* p. x.

5. Ibid., p. ix.
6. Ibid., p. x.
7. Ibid., p. ix.
8. *Mori Ōgai zenshū* (Tokyo: Iwanami shoten, 1972), vol. 4, p. 46.
9. Ibid., vol. 4, pp. 52-53.
10. Since this writing, a meticulous and touching study of Io by Edwin McClellan has appeared, *Woman in the Crested Kimono* (New Haven: Yale University Press, 1985), which sheds light on the whole period.
11. *Mori Ōgai zenshū*, vol. 4, p. 233.
12. Sartre, *The Family Idiot*, p. ix.

CHAPTER 8: The Theme of Pilgrimage in Japanese Literature

1. See his article "Spent Arrows and First Buddings," *New Yorker,* 3 January 1983, pp. 66-70.
2. Shiga Naoya, *A Dark Night's Passing*, trans. Edwin McClellan (Tokyo and New York: Kodansha International, 1976), p. 197.
3. Kawabata Yasunari, *Snow Country*, trans. Edward Seidensticker (New York: Alfred A. Knopf, 1957), p. 155.
4. For useful definitions of *aware*, see various entries in Robert Brower and Earl Miner, *Japanese Court Poetry* (Stanford: Stanford University Press, 1961), as well as Hisamatsu Sen'ichi, *The Vocabulary of Japanese Literary Aesthetics* (Tokyo: Center for East Asian Cultural Studies, 1963), and in Ueda Makoto, *Literary and Art Theories in Japan* (Cleveland: The Press of Western Reserve University, 1967).
5. This citation is taken from an explanatory passage in Hilda Kato, "The *Mumyōshō* of Kamo no Chōmei and Its Significance in Japanese Literature," *Monumenta Nipponica* 23, 3-4 (1969): 325. Two complete English versions of the preface, with annotations, have recently appeared, included in complete translations of the *Kokinshū*. See *Kokin Wakashū, The First Imperial Anthology of Japanese Poetry*, trans. Helen Craig McCullough (Stanford: Stanford University Press, 1985), pp. 3-13, and *Kokinshū, a Collection of Poems Ancient and Modern*, trans. Laurel Rasplica Rodd with Mary Catherine Henkenius (Princeton: Princeton University Press, 1984).
6. See Earl Miner, *Japanese Poetic Diaries* (Berkeley: University of California Press, 1969), p. 67.
7. Ibid.
8. Murasaki Shikibu, *The Tale of Genji*, trans. Edward Seidensticker (New York: Alfred A. Knopf, 1980), p. 437.
9. Kamo no Chōmei, *Mumyōshō*, in Kato, "The *Mumyōshō* of Kamo no Chōmei," p. 398.

10. Ibid., p. 398.

11. Ibid., p. 409.

12. Matsuo Bashō, *The Narrow Road to the Deep North and Other Travel Sketches*, trans. Nobuyuki Yuasa (Baltimore: Penguin Classics, 1966), p. 28.

13. Ibid., p. 33.

14. For a thorough and highly imaginative treatment of Bashō's artistic strategies and their development in his work, see Eleanor Kerkham, *Images of the Hermit Traveller: A Study on Bashō's Early Prose Works* (forthcoming).

15. Kitagawa Hiroshi and Bruce Tsuchida, trans., *The Tale of the Heike* (Tokyo: University of Tokyo Press, 1975), p. 598.

16. Ibid., p. 600.

17. Ibid., p. 601.

18. Ivan Morris, trans., *As I Crossed a Bridge of Dreams: Recollections of a Woman in Eleventh Century Japan* (New York: Dial Press, 1971), p. 62.

19. Donald Keene, *Anthology of Japanese Literature* (New York: Grove Press, 1955), p. 346.

20. Ibid., p. 347.

21. Miner, *Japanese Poetic Diaries*, p. 74.

22. Ibid.

23. In his critical writings on the *nō*, Zeami maintained that the rhythm of all art was derived from nature and involved a progression from slow to fast. He used this principle for the basis of his *jo-ha-kyū* (introduction–development–fast finale) rhythmical structure in the *nō*.

24. Murasaki, *The Tale of Genji*, pp. 353–354.

25. Helen Craig McCullough, trans., *The Tales of Ise: Lyrical Episodes from Tenth-century Japan* (Stanford: Stanford University Press, 1968), p. 101.

26. Ibid., p. 102.

27. Miner, *Japanese Poetic Diaries*, pp. 176–177.

Some Further Readings on
France and Japan

The connections in the cultural field between France and Japan since the Meiji period are important and complex. There is yet to appear in any language, as far as I know, a systematic and synthetic account of these various mutual influences. The scholarly communities in both countries have addressed the subject, but within the kind of intellectual and academic framework familiar to them. As the cultural systems of perception do not necessarily mesh, the significance of certain connections and the development of particular lines of thought have yet to be fully explicated.

In Japan a number of useful studies of literary influences in the field of comparative literature have been made. Many of these accounts record what books were translated into Japanese from the French, what works Japanese writers and painters read or saw, and how they may have adapted these new influences into their own oeuvre. Useful in such contexts, these studies do not set out to probe the metamorphosis of mentalities that lie at the root of the mutual attraction between the two civilizations. This phenomenon is best observed directly in the written statements of the artists themselves, as I have tried to indicate in my treatment of Shimazaki Tōson. There are other Japanese writers who reflect on the French experience in those terms, among them the novelist Serizawa Kōjirō and the artist Fujita Tsuguji, whose various essays reveal a remarkable self-awareness of the nature and attraction of these two competing cultural systems. Two recent publications in Japan have begun to suggest how appropriate lines of comparative inquiry might proceed. The first of them, written in English, by Sawada Suketarō, is entitled *Little Hanako* (Nagoya: Chūnichi Publishing Company, 1984) and provides a fascinating account of Rodin's Japanese model, who, among other things, provided the subject matter for Mori Ōgai's 1910 story, "Hanako." The second, *La Japonaise* by Yajima Midori (Tokyo: Ushio shuppan, 1983), is a biography of the novelist Yamada Kiku. Perhaps best known in English-speaking countries for her novel *Woman of Beauty*, written in 1953, Yamada spent a good deal of her life in France and understood much of the appeal that French culture held out for sophisticated Japanese during the interwar period.

In the field of the visual arts, where the connections between France and Japan have been particularly close, a number of useful publications provide good information on the effect of French painting and sculpture on the work of Japanese artists. One in particular might be noted here, a catalogue published in 1983 by the Bridgestone Museum in Tokyo entitled *Nihon kindai yōga no ishi to Furansu: L'Académie du Japon moderne et les pientres français*, with essays in both French and Japanese on the training of Japanese painters in the various French public and private academies from the 1880s through the period that ended with World War I. There is a remarkable amount of information provided, including some letters and other documents that shed useful light on how the Japanese responded to French civilization.

In France there has been less work done in this area than might be expected. This is surely at least partially because in the French humanistic tradition, the study of Japan is generally approached in the same fashion as that of Greece or Rome. Elements in her ancient civilization are examined with skill and care, but modern and contemporary Japan are not considered an altogether appropriate subject for sustained scholarly inquiry. These attitudes are changing, and the present generation of younger scholars is beginning to examine modern Japanese literature with skill and insight.

Nevertheless, the French have not examined Japan's French connection until very recently, when in 1986 the Centre Pompidou in Paris staged a remarkable exhibition, "Japan des Avant Gardes 1910–1970," which included examples of painting, architecture, photography, literature, theatre, and dance. The inspiration of the French example in the creation of a genuine modern Japanese art was made strikingly clear in the exhibition, and hopefully the success of this endeavor will stimulate more research. A large and beautifully prepared catalogue is available, and it contains as well a most useful bibliography (Paris: Editions du Centre Pompidou, 1986). The previous year, an exhibit of Japanese paintings done in Paris during the period 1890–1940 was shown at the Musée Carnavalet, entitled "Paris vu par les Artistes Japonais." The exhibition provided a useful chronicle of the shifting vision from generation to generation of the artistic Japanese sensibility as it confronted France and French culture. The catalogue, written by the staff of the *Asahi Shimbun* in Tokyo and published in French, has a limited amount of space for text, but provides a useful introduction to the subject.

The subject has also begun to attract a certain amount of attention in the United States. Masao Mayoshi was perhaps the first to describe the psychology of the European pilgrimage for the Japanese in his chapter on Mori Ōgai in his *Accomplices of Silence* (Berkeley: University of California Press, 1974). Ellen Conant has provided a complex and fascinating picture of the early years of these cultural encounters in her excellent study "The French Connection: Emile Guimet's Mission to Japan, a Cultural Context for *Japonisme*," in Hilary Conroy, Sandra T. W. Davis, and Wayne Patterson, ed., *Japan in Transition: Thought and Action in the Meiji Era* (Rutherford, N.J.: Fairleigh Dickinson University Press, 1984), pp. 113–146.

Steven Light's book *Shūzō Kuki and Jean-Paul Sartre: Influence and Counter-Influence in the Early History of Existential Phenomenology* (Carbondale and Edwardsville: Southern Illinois University Press, 1987) sketches out congruences of thought and inspiration shared by Kuki and Sartre when they knew each other as young men in Europe. Sartre's example in terms of contemporary Japanese thinking forms an important element in John Whittier Treat's article *"Hiroshima noto* and Oe Kenzaburō's Existentialist Other," in the *Harvard Journal of Asiatic Studies* 47, no. 1 (June 1986): 97–136. Finally, the lengthy catalogue, *Paris in Japan,* prepared by Takashina Shūji, Gerald Bolas, and myself for the 1987–1988 art exhibition "Paris in Japan," and published by Washington University in St. Louis, provides a number of art works and documents that help show the reciprocal enthusiasms that drew the two civilizations together.

Index of Historical Personalities, Authors, and Literary Terms

145

About the Author

J. Thomas Rimer received his doctorate from Columbia University and is currently chair of the Department of Hebrew and East Asian Languages and Literatures at the University of Maryland, College Park. He has a wide range of interests in Japanese literature and culture, including the visual arts, and recently coauthored the exhibition catalogue *Paris in Japan,* which illustrates Japanese encounters with European art in the early years of the twentieth century. Among his other publications are *Traditions in Modern Japanese Fiction: An Introduction* and *The Way of Acting: The Theatre Writings of Tadashi Suzuki.*

HAWAI Production Notes

This book was designed by Roger Eggers.
Composition and paging were done on the
Quadex Composing System and typesetting
on the Compugraphic 8400 by the design
and production staff of University of
Hawaii Press.

The text typeface is Baskerville and the
display typeface is Compugraphic Palatino.

Offset presswork and binding were done by
Vail-Ballou Press, Inc. Text paper is
Glatfelter Offset Vellum, basis 50.